Media Industry Studies

SHORT INTRODUCTIONS

Nicholas Abercrombie, *Sociology*
Michael Bury, *Health and Illness*
Raewyn Connell and Rebecca Pearse, *Gender,* 3rd edition
Hartley Dean, *Social Policy,* 3rd edition
Lena Dominelli, *Introducing Social Work*
Jonathan Gray and Amanda D. Lotz, *Television Studies,* 2nd edition
Jeffrey Haynes, *Development Studies*
Stuart Henry, with Lindsay M. Howard, *Social Deviance,* 2nd edition
Daniel Herbert, Amanda D. Lotz, and Aswin Punathambekar, *Media Industry Studies*
Stephanie Lawson, *International Relations,* 3rd edition
Ronald L. Mize, *Latina/o Studies*
Chris Rojek, *Cultural Studies*
Mary Romero, *Introducing Intersectionality*
Karen Wells, *Childhood Studies*

Media Industry Studies

Daniel Herbert, Amanda D. Lotz, and Aswin Punathambekar

polity

First published in 2020 by Polity Press

Polity Press
65 Bridge Street
Cambridge CB2 1UR, UK

Polity Press
101 Station Landing
Suite 300
Medford, MA 02155, USA

ISBN-13: 978-1-5095-3777-8 (hardback)
ISBN-13: 978-1-5095-3778-5 (paperback)

A catalogue record for this book is available from the British Library.

Library of Congress Cataloging-in-Publication Data

Names: Herbert, Daniel, 1974- author. | Lotz, Amanda D., 1974- author. | Punathambekar, Aswin, author.
Title: Media industry studies / Daniel Herbert, Amanda D. Lotz and Aswin Punathambekar.
Description: Cambridge, UK ; Medford, MA : Polity, 2020. | Series: Short introductions | Includes bibliographical references and index. | Summary: "This text provides the roadmap to the vibrant area of Media Industry studies"-- Provided by publisher.
Identifiers: LCCN 2019036734 (print) | LCCN 2019036735 (ebook) | ISBN 9781509537778 (hardback) | ISBN 9781509537785 (paperback) | ISBN 9781509537792 (epub)
Subjects: LCSH: Mass media--Study and teaching.
Classification: LCC P91.3 .H46 2020 (print) | LCC P91.3 (ebook) | DDC 384--dc23
LC record available at https://lccn.loc.gov/2019036734
LC ebook record available at https://lccn.loc.gov/2019036735

Typeset in 10 on 12pt Sabon
by Fakenham Prepress Solutions, Fakenham, Norfolk NR21 8NL
Printed and bound in Great Britain by CPI Group (UK) Ltd, Croydon

For further information on Polity, visit our website: politybooks.com

For our mentors, peers, and students

Contents

Acknowledgments

This book grew out of many conversations, both among the three of us and many shared with others. They were often conversations in which we tried to pin down what it is we do and how we do it. While these pages formalize the deeper and systematic conversation we've shared, we intend it as the continuation of a conversation. We thank those of you who have engaged with us in this conversation, formally and informally, often as our mentors and students, but many also as collaborators and peers.

This precise book developed on the 5th and half floor of North Quad over the past few years. Our conversations were deeply influenced by colleagues Paddy Scannell, Megan Ankerson, Katherine Sender, Sarah Murray, and Yeidy Rivero. Much was also worked out in conversations with students including Jimmy Draper, Annemarie Navar-Gill, Kitior Ngu, and in the space of the Media Studies Research Workshop as well as the multiple iterations of the "Analyzing Media Industries" seminar.

Our uncertainties sent us asking questions of others. Many thanks to Janet Staiger, Joseph Turow, Graham Murdock, Eileen Meehan, Michele Hilmes, and Philip Schlesinger for their assistance in tracing the history of the field. The list of peers and collaborators who helped us to shape our sense of the field is too long to recount, but thanks to C. W. Anderson, Nitin Govil, David Hesmondhalgh, Lee Marshall, Jeremy Morris, John Thompson, and Nikki Usher for assistance with areas outside our central expertise.

Our sincere appreciation to Ramon Lobato for reading an early draft and offering feedback that challenged us to do better. Thanks as well for feedback from Sriram Mohan, Anna Sampson, Michael Wayne, and our most excellent research assistant, Rae Moors. We are also thankful for the considerable support of Polity's reviewers, and Mary Savigar, Ellen MacDonald-Kramer, and the Polity editorial and production team.

And finally, our thanks to our families for cheerfully putting up with phone calls and Skype conversations at odd hours and other absences required to bring this to completion.

Introduction

"I want to study YouTube as a media industry," announces a new student. "OK, what kind of study?" There are numerous potential research projects one could design with a focus on YouTube as a major site of media production and circulation. Or, YouTube could serve as a case from which to make broader claims about various sectors and practices of digital media industries and their intricate links with established screen industries in an era of seemingly unfettered global connectivity.

One potential study would focus on the people who make YouTube videos; not just the creators and influencers with millions of followers worldwide, but also the many millions of people who create and circulate videos across an astonishing range of genres. There are many questions that we could pose about their practice. It would also be possible to study the content moderators whose daily, routine work involves scanning hundreds, if not thousands, of videos that have been flagged by automated systems for content review for potential violation of YouTube standards of acceptability. Or, delving a bit deeper, you could focus attention on the engineers who design the content moderation algorithms. You could do interviews, observe them in their roles for a period of time, attend industry events designed for professionals in the digital technology and media industries, and try to understand the broader work culture within which a range of people go about their routines. There are many ways to study any of these groups of media workers and many sound reasons to do so.

While a focus on specific *individuals and their roles* within YouTube and its specific *production culture* is valuable, you could also examine

YouTube as an *organization* and explore questions related to its particular strategies as a social media company that circulates videos. Such a study would aim to build knowledge of the broader forces that shape the behavior of social media companies, such as their interactions with advertisers and their policies for dealing with the people who create the content on their services. A study of YouTube as an organization might build knowledge about how social media companies operate generally, but would do so by constructing a detailed understanding of how YouTube's strategies, practices, and aims lead it to create particular social media capabilities and limit others. It might address how the strategies for YouTube relate to broader activities of parent company Google.

Yet another approach would be a study of the logics of social media industries writ large. This type of study would aim to identify the regulatory, technological, economic, and cultural features of the playing field upon which social media companies operate, how they contribute to the social media experiences users engage, and the cultural relations that result. You could also approach YouTube from a "textual" angle and analyze how a combination of industrial factors may have facilitated an entire range of web series that challenge mainstream media industries' representations of marginalized and minority communities. Finally, there is also the possibility of adopting a macro-level perspective to examine how YouTube negotiates different regulatory regimes across nations, or how it relies on trade and tax policies to maximize its earnings in an explanation of where it locates its server farms or corporate offices, how it responds to varying regulatory regimes across its multinational reach, and how these practices also shape the social media experiences it makes available and denies its users.

The scenario that we have sketched here of how one might study YouTube as a media industry points to a variety of sites and approaches. Needless to say, any such study would spiral outward to engage with questions and issues to do with media infrastructures, devices, the politics of datafication and algorithmic curation, convergence between digital media companies and established screen industries, exploitative labor practices, state censorship, pirate media networks, and so on. There is enormous variation in the questions that we could pose in any particular domain of a social media company like YouTube. Discerning the right research question is an important part of the process – and actually, the question you aim to answer is likely the strongest guide to the method to use and the scale of the study. Related to that research question, what is the broader scholarly conversation to which you aim to contribute? What are its key dilemmas? Do you think there might be evidence that contradicts the existing thinking? Do you seek to apply existing theory to a new media industry context? Establishing a research question and the conversation you are engaging in is crucial to identifying what method to deploy and the most relevant theories for interpreting findings.

If this is our answer to one seemingly straightforward question from a student, then it may appear well-nigh impossible to compose a Short Introduction *to Media Industry Studies* in the following pages. By some accounts, media industry studies burst forth around 2009 and rapidly grew into a subfield with a dedicated peer-reviewed scholarly journal, thriving interest groups in multiple scholarly organizations, and was the focus of a filled-to-capacity, standalone international conference in 2018. This Short Introduction explores the formation of media industry studies, as it has tenuously cohered as a subfield in the last decade by teasing apart its long and diverse intellectual past: What theories and methods have scholars in different disciplines and traditions used in their analysis of media industries? What broader social and political forces have drawn scholarly attention to the workings of the media industries at different historical conjunctures? Does the study of media industries take very different forms in different national and cultural contexts? If media industries have always been key sites of analysis for media and communication scholars, why does "media industry studies" cohere in the late twentieth and early twenty-first century? Given the increasing fragmentation of media studies, what are the intellectual and political stakes in naming and legitimizing it as a subfield to media study?

In addressing these and other questions, we identify some of the central questions of this research as well as uninterrogated assumptions. This account does not encompass all types of media industry studies, but *explores the questions and methods of those that do so with a particular interest in understanding and examining media industries due to their role in the production and circulation of culture*. There are a variety of theoretical traditions and central areas of inquiry within the *Media Industry Studies* we discuss, and there are also other approaches to studying media industries that are not addressed or incorporated extensively because questions of culture figure less centrally in their inquiry. A Short Introduction obviously does not pretend to offer a complete treatment of the topics and themes it discusses; for this, we hope that readers will turn to the primary sources on which we draw here.

Several other recent books offer insights into the "what, why, and how?" of media industry studies. *Media Industries: History, Theory, and Method* (2009), edited by Jennifer Holt and Alisa Perren, helped define media industry studies as a coherent but interdisciplinary area of research. Their collection features numerous essays by leading scholars about many of the key questions and concerns that animate media industry studies, as well as various theories and methods scholars use in addressing them. Our Short Introduction takes a similarly wide-ranging approach to defining media industry studies, but offers readers a more synthesized analysis of how different scholars have engaged in media industries research across multiple sites and scales. *Understanding Media Industries* (2e, 2014) by Timothy Havens and Amanda D. Lotz provides an introduction to the operation of media industries and offers a framework that highlights the interconnected practices within their operation. This text might be helpful for triggering ideas about the range of topics and issues that a media industry study might encompass, but it attends only slightly to the underlying theories and scholarly conversations at the heart of media industry studies. For that, David Hesmondhalgh's *The Cultural Industries* (4e, 2019), is an essential read. First published in 2003, *The Cultural Industries* provided a formative text for many who began their research careers at the start of the century. It expansively details many of the key analytic frameworks and theories and has been extensively updated to keep pace with the new issues developing in an era of social and internet-distributed media. An essay by Havens, Lotz, and Serra Tinic (2009) lays out "critical media industry studies" as a research approach. Now more than a decade old, that essay helped name and provide coherence to the budding subfield shared with Holt and Perren and research about production studies examined in detail in Chapter 3. We take advantage of ten years of research development – and the additional space offered by a book-length examination – to identify how macro-scale research of the political economy upon which media industries operate can be contextually grounded and culturally informed.

In terms of how to do media industry research, Matthew Freeman's *Industrial Approaches to Media: A Methodological Gateway to Industry Study* (2016) and Chris Paterson's edited collection of essays *Advancing Media Production Research* (2016) detail many of the research methods that characterize contemporary media industries research, as well as many of the practical and philosophical issues raised by these different methods. Like Freeman, this Short Introduction provides extensive discussion of previous scholarship as a means of sorting through the larger questions and methods pertaining to media industries scholarship. Our book supports its examination of how to do media industry studies by using examples of research and tracing the relationship of methods and research questions by illustration. This book goes into significant historical depth in tracing the growth of media industries research and, just as importantly, examines cases from across many different media industries, while Freeman's offers practical methodological tips.

Defining Media Industries

Before we assemble and narrativize origin stories for media industry studies, we need to ask what, in the first place, are media industries? Media economists have defined media industries as those sectors that make, manage, and circulate intellectual property (Doyle, 2013), which has led others to consider them as "copyright" industries (Wikström, 2013). The borders of media industries have long been nebulous – sometimes considered part of a larger sector of cultural industries or creative industries that include sport and fashion – though are most commonly explored as discrete entities such as the film, newspaper, television, gaming, or music industries. The development of internet distribution and social media companies over the past two decades has exacerbated our uncertainty about boundaries and defining character-istics of media. For instance, while companies such as Facebook and YouTube manage circulation, they have also begun producing original content. Moreover, they often make intellectual property claims in relation to proprietary algorithmic systems. Many of the concepts and methods developed for studying established media industries are thus helpful for investigating digital media industries as well.

We can also follow the lead of media economists who point to distinctive features of media industries such as high first-copy costs, their status as public goods, and low-to-no marginal costs as characteristics that distinguish this sector from other industries and lead to uncommon industrial tendencies. These features steer media industries towards particular strategies and behaviors unlike a more general array of indus-tries commonly theorized by economic and business literatures. At the same time, media scholars have long argued that the *cultural* role played by media, despite their status as industrial products, makes it crucial for us to examine their modes of production and circulation (Hall, 1980; du Gay et al., 1997; Hesmondhalgh, 2019). Consequently, the intel-lectual history and approaches to the study of media industries that we explore here mostly focuses on scholarship that holds together economic, political, and cultural dimensions of media.

Our view is that understanding the emergence of media industry studies, the questions it asks, and the methods it uses, does not require rigid delimitation of acceptable objects of study; the aims of study – of why scholars are compelled to examine the workings of media industries – are more salient. Consequently, we don't provide a fixed definition of which industries "count" as media industries, and allow that the wide-ranging methodological and conceptual frameworks of media industry study might prove helpful in understanding other industries as well. Indeed, some of the scholarship cited in this book was not likely considered as media industry studies by those doing the research. These cases demonstrate the methodological range of media industries' research while offering important insights into industry workings. We find that looking beyond one's home discipline can often be fruitful and, in the case of media industry studies, is often necessary.

In this regard, we take our cue from Nitin Govil (2013) and John Thornton Caldwell (2013), who have urged scholars to reflect on what, in the first place, constitutes an "industry." Pointing to capitalist media industries' capacity to narrate stories and develop theories about their own operations, Caldwell argues that we need to be highly reflexive about the object of our research and not fall into the trap of imagining the "industry as a clean, self-evident sphere or as a bounded site for research" (2013, 157). In a similar vein, Govil's account of the Indian film sector's struggles to be recognized as a formal "industry" encourages us to look beyond the established media industries and "broaden the range of practices that count as industry" (2013, 176). One of our goals in this book, therefore, is to reflect on how various scholars have defined the contours of an industry, or a particular domain within a given industry, and how their decisions shape research questions, methods, and interpretive frameworks.

What is this Media Industry Studies?

Political economy of communication, cultural studies, sociology, media economics, new film history, and organization and business studies have long been the homes of those scholars who have asked and examined questions about media industries. We don't seek to supplant any of these intellectual trajectories with what we categorize here as media industry studies. But we do seek to identify and encourage the crosspollination of studies of media industries across these different traditions with their differing intellectual priorities, and believe that demarcating media industry studies might be a helpful way to do so. As evident in the intellectual history of media industry studies that we trace in Chapter 1, scholars identifying their work within traditions of political economy of communication, cultural studies, and new film history were often animated by similar interests and concerns, but the partitioning of academic fields and focus on discrepant media in different fields led these conversations to be more siloed than shared.

We understand media industry studies as a component of the broader field of media studies. Michele Hilmes (2018) defines critical media studies as centered "on the critical analysis of *texts* – not texts in isolation, but as they are produced by industries and institutions, and received by audiences and societies" (xii). At its core, the media industry studies we articulate are focused on the critical analysis of *how individuals, institutions, and industries produce and circulate cultural forms in historically and geographically contextualized ways*. We would broaden from Hilmes's focus on the critical analysis of "texts" to include the routines, norms, and infrastructural conditions in which *cultural* dynamics are worked out as likewise central to study, and include studies of media making and circulation as cultures in their own right. There are other intellectual traditions for studying media industries, of course, that aren't driven by concerns about culture. We do acknowledge a few of these here, particularly in cases where they offer tools that can enrich a media studies-style approach to media industries.

As the book's object of analysis, we understand media industry studies as a big tent that encompasses the research that explores the creation and circulation of media across the spectrum of micro to macro perspectives by identifying and examining industrial practices and analyzing their consequences. It explores the operation of power across and within global and national regimes, business sectors, labor communities, or within media organizations. It adheres to the premise that *how* media texts are made, promoted, and made available shapes *what* is made, and that the circulation of bits of culture further infuses them with meaning and significance that is then negotiated through practices of consumption. We do not have a list of topics, approaches, or methods that qualify as media industries, but engage with those whose questions converse with these aims, regardless of whether they study audiovisual, audio, photo, or word-based media. We believe the approaches and methods of media industry studies can encompass media that use analog and digital distribution technologies, as well as the industrial formations of social media. Perhaps the greatest uncertainty comes from the word industry itself, as the increasing availability of the tools of media creation and circulation make it in unclear at what point media become industrialized.

We deliberately draw the boundaries of media industry studies more broadly than is typically done. Much of the work associated with media industry studies of the last decade has taken audiovisual industries as their focus. While such studies are the home for our own work, we argue that focus risks missing insights about media and culture produced by studies that have located a home in sociology, popular music, game, and journalism studies. Instead of drawing boundaries around media forms or asserting an unassailable distinction between the cultural functions of "information" and "entertainment," we believe studies of all these forms of media are united in the type of media studies that scholars like Hilmes articulate. Of course, the specificity of industrial norms typically requires us to ground studies in a particular industry but, in terms of intellectual context, we imagine media industry studies to encompass a broad range of cultural production because it is the case that, for instance, a study on how a journalist negotiates newsroom practices to get editorial support for a story might have more to offer a study of how directors negotiate ideas to achieve film studio support than has been assumed.

It may be that some disagree about their work being described as media industry studies, although we hope not, and that others find our refusal to draw firm boundaries problematic. Our sense is that the current moment of inquiry and fluctuation in media industry operations warrants synthesis and crosspollination over turf marking and siloed conversations. When the three of us were students in graduate programs in the United States, regular course offerings on media industries were rare. But over the past ten to fifteen years, we have collaborated with many scholars who have played key roles in the development of this subfield. We also find ourselves mentoring several doctoral students whose work comfortably transverses the boundaries we were taught, and we follow their lead toward broadening the subfield further in the years to come.

Chapter 1 expands bits and pieces of a lineage of inquiry that we have discerned, or has been described by our mentors, into a first draft of an account that illustrates a wide range of influences that will certainly be refined in the decades to come. Although this subfield remains nascent, a more detailed topographic map of it can help those trying to place their own inquiries within this expanding and amorphous intellectual terrain. We hope our account sparks conversations that bring even greater detail to the influences shaping the subfield, as such an account could be a book in its own right.

We also seek to identify blind spots and challenges for media industry studies in the coming decades. Where possible, we attend to issues of race, ethnicity, class, gender, sexuality, geography, and other forms of difference that structure and inform the operations of the media industries, as well as those that structure the availability of media and communication technologies. Media industries continually produce and reinforce these and other forms of difference for society at large in the films, television programs, popular music, social media services, journalism, and other media that they create and circulate. Attending to these issues entails reflecting on the relatively marginal influence of critical race theory, feminist studies, and postcolonial studies in informing and shaping conceptual and empirical research agendas in media industry studies so far.

Criteria and Organization

Our goal of synthesizing disparate traditions of media industry studies and a multiplicity of media industries negated a common organization of books such as this that arrange chapters by industry. Chapter 1 builds the case that the study of media industries has a long and diverse intellectual lineage, and uses a chronological account of key scholarship that has explored how media industries produce and circulate texts and the cultural roles and power they encompass. We narrate that story in greater depth and suggest more synthesis than commonly recognized, though confining this account to a single chapter limits its comprehensiveness. Intellectual traditions such as critical theory and political economy of communication provide a deep history of thought regarding the intersection of culture and industry, and more generally of cultural production under the conditions of industrial capitalism. Exploring these traditions of inquiry allows us to trace influences and cross fertilization evident with hindsight. Our aim is not to rigidly or prescriptively delimit the boundaries of a proper approach to the study of media industries or a single intellectual lineage. Rather, we illustrate the influences and the strengths of various traditions and methods that engage centrally in questions of cultural production, as well as some that do so tangentially, but offer tools and insight that can be deployed for cultural analysis.

Chapters 2 through 6 are organized based on what we roughly conceive of as different "levels" of analysis or scales of study, moving in a general way from the micro to the macro. We use this structure in order to organize the variation of media industry studies and intend the levels merely to sort sites of study and explicitly *not* to suggest any hierarchical relationship. These classifications are messy and imperfect, and the point here is not a precise taxonomy, but to organize a broad array of scholarship that can otherwise seem too disorderly to contemplate. As Lotz and Newcomb (2012, 72) write in the chapter that establishes this heuristic: "The most effective production research will indicate an awareness of the multiple levels and seek to identify the interdependence of the influences, even if focusing upon particular cases, settings, and systems."

Another way we might understand the levels is as offering different vantage points, in the same way that the surface of the earth appears differently from space, from a jet at 30,000 feet, a helicopter, a tall building, or when one is standing on the ground. Havens, Lotz, and Tinic (2009, 239) used this metaphor to argue for the mid-level approach of critical media industry studies, and we add additional levels of focus through our consideration in this book. As we illustrate throughout, no level is better than the others; rather, different questions can be answered based on the evidence available and relative to the scale of the study. A focus on different "levels" – however loose or overlapping they may appear – enables us to demonstrate connections *across* different industries and to examine examples from different regions of the world. Ideally, the cases we discuss can serve as inspiration for a range of research projects on new and distinct objects of study.

The levels heuristic guides our criteria for selecting examples in Chapters 2 through 6, followed by the aim of drawing from an array of media industries and of providing an account of more than just Western media industries and scholarship. Our primary focus is to use existing scholarship to tease apart the types of questions media industries scholarship has asked, the methods used to answer those questions, and the claims that can be produced. Individually and collectively we have criticisms of some of the research included here; nor would we claim our own scholarship to be exemplary and without limitation. As a book motivated to encourage contemplation about the craft of media industry scholarship, it aims for readers to identify the inevitable trade-offs related to scope, method, and access, rather than building our account to create some sort of canon. Consequently, we often select studies primarily because they discuss method explicitly, or can be brought into conversation with other research to illuminate a bigger point. We look forward to the comprehensive literature reviews others might write.

Chapter 2 begins with the most micro-level scale, with scholarship that examines people who work in media and their industrial roles. Chapter 3 focuses on research about production cultures and is followed by an investigation of scholarship about organizations in Chapter 4. Research focused on the industry scale organizes Chapter 5 and, finally, Chapter 6 explores macro contexts of national and multinational political economy. These sites of study function almost like stacking dolls in that people make up organizations, organizations make up industries, and the behavior of industries is circumscribed by the political economy in which they operate. Notably, in Chapter 6 we are using the term political economy as distinct from its use in the intellectual history of Chapter 1, as critical political economy and its typical use in media studies. The global political economy – as the organizing topic of Chapter 6 – is the landscape within which all media industries operate. Questions about trade, tariffs, and labor common to this level can be examined through many different approaches, not only those associated with critical political economy. Likewise, a critical political economy approach can be used at any of the other levels of study.

Each chapter explores a range of scholarship characteristic of that level, in order to identify the key questions examined and the assortment of methods deployed in such analysis. Media industry studies use an array of methods and evidence, including industry and government data, archives of media organizations and individuals, trade publications, industry events, interviews, observation and, in some cases, participant observation and long-term ethnographic fieldwork. The aim of this chapter organization is to integrate exploration of what has been studied and learned, alongside how those insights were achieved. We show that particular types of questions and insight correlate with the level of analysis, although similar methods are deployed across every level.

There are many other ways in which we could have organized this book. For example, we could have structured chapters by medium, geographic region, or chronology of scholarship. We opted for "levels" because this organization best allows us to focus on the different types of research questions that media industries scholarship has asked and the ways it has gone about answering them. Moreover, this organizational structure helps us move across contexts and show that theoretical developments that emerge out of a study in Nigeria, for instance, can and should inform scholarship elsewhere. We recognize the problem of building largely on scholarship rooted in the north Atlantic, Anglophone contexts, and instead endeavored to draw connections that transcend national boundaries.

We also very explicitly eschewed a "by industry" approach because if we were to point to a notable weakness of media industry studies, it is that it only engages in multi- or cross-industry examination or conversation on rare occasions (e.g. Curtin, 2007; Elkins, 2019; Herbert, Lotz, and Marshall, 2019; Holt, 2011; Punathambekar, 2013). While the particular dynamics of the music industry are obviously different from that of film, an intellectual enterprise such as media industry studies should aspire to identifying ideas or theories that offer insight to multiple industries. Similarly, we embrace an understanding of media industries that does not bind them to particular distribution technology. Whether albums, cassettes, downloads, or streaming services, the study of music industries – or any other medium – should not be artificially segmented into analog and digital industry versions. Despite initial expectations, much of what were once believed to be "new media" are clearly understandable as written word, audio, or audiovisual media industries that are disrupted and reconfigured by digital technologies. We hope that an organization by level will help reveal which questions the body of media industry studies scholarship has answered, which methodological tools have been particularly useful for such questions, and will inspire scholars to pose new questions and imagine new ways of answering them. Indeed, it is precisely this range of methods and topics that we believe makes media industry studies an exciting and fruitful area of research, and which this Short Introduction seeks to clarify.

1

The Origins of Media Industry Studies

Having sketched out the overarching goals of this book, we turn our attention now to outlining an intellectual history of this new subfield. Although media industry studies has been instrumental over the last fifteen years or so in bringing a new prominence to matters of media production and circulation, industry dynamics and practices, and capitalism and cultural production, it is by no means unique in its academic concerns with the subjects of media industries and institutions. It is also, not surprisingly, methodologically and conceptually indebted to a range of both earlier and more recent developments in media theory as well as scholarship in closely allied fields, including critical race theory, feminist studies, and postcolonial studies. Our primary goal in this chapter, however, is to situate media industry studies within a global history of media studies and in doing so, to outline key theoretical influences and points of departure.

The study of media industries has always been part of the examination of the power that media wield on cultures and societies. Not surprisingly, the operations of media industries have particularly attracted academic attention during moments of dramatic change – whether socio-political or technological. This research has been rooted in different disciplines at different moments and in different places – sociology, communication, political economy, cultural studies, film history, critical theory – and, consequently, has not been regarded as being part of a larger and coherent intellectual enterprise. In fact, through much of the late twentieth century, we can trace multiple, and even competing, strands of media industry study. The formation of a coherent enterprise identifying as media industry studies at the end of the first decade of the twenty-first century builds on the diverse work that came before.

An early suggestion of the need for a media industry perspective can be found in a 1991 article by Jeremy Tunstall, who dates the first macro industrial approach of media research to Max Weber in 1910. Roots of media industry studies can be identified throughout the 1920s, when scholars turned to the workings of the cultural industries in order to answer questions about culture and its fraught links with the economy, politics, and society. Although predominantly remembered as early textual and audience effects studies, the Payne Fund studies in the United States (1929 to 1932) that examined the effect of movies on children sought an *industrial* solution through the creation of a set of moral guidelines known as the Hays Code. During this decade in Western Europe, the Institute for Social Research was established in Germany (1923) and became the center for the cultural turn within Marxist thinking that explored how the power of culture might explain the acceptance of class-based subjugation. Thinkers associated with the Frankfurt School examined the social and cultural significance of film and music, among other media and arts, and included analyses of production, textual form, and audiences in their accounts.

The more commonly acknowledged starting point for media industry study is the 1940s, with the continued efforts to explain propaganda and its effects in society. Paddy Scannell (2007) notes that Paul Lazarsfeld and Robert Merton, who are commonly associated with the establishment of US effects and persuasion research, established a "critique of the media as soft disciplinary agents of the economic and social status quo" in postwar America (72). Two relevant research trajectories emerged at this time. Lazarsfeld built from the concerns about media effects that were the basis of the Payne Fund studies, but also engaged in a considerable amount of media industries research, in this case in the service of government and corporate sponsors. The trajectory of research Lazarsfeld inspired has been distinguished as "administrative" research because of its aims in advancing the industry's knowledge about itself for strategic purposes.

This administrative tradition contrasted with the critical perspective toward media industries found in the research of the Frankfurt School, and most famously in Theodor Adorno and Max Horkheimer's 1944 manifesto on "The Culture Industry" – although there was co-mingling among administrative and critical researchers at the time. "The Culture Industry" explicitly critiqued the phenomenon of mass culture, which was understood as culture created for the masses, not the culture created of the people, and used industrialized methods of mass production and sales. Importantly, as early as the 1940s – if not the 1920s – we see scholars recognizing the power of media in society not simply in the films, radio broadcasts, and media of the time – but looking to the creators of media, be they individuals or institutions, and seeking to understand industrial motivations to produce particular types of content.

Two notable studies from the 1940s examined the workers and internal business structures of the American film industry from socio-logical and anthropological perspectives in order to better understand how work practices and production cultures might impact the form and content of movies. Leo Rosten's 1941 book *Hollywood: The Movie Colony, the Movie Makers* grew out of the author's sociological training and interest in the social effect of movies, as well as his experience as a screenwriter in the late 1930s. The book draws upon copious empirical research, including "interviews, questionnaires ... government statistics, market data, and casual observation of media elites" (Sullivan, 2009). Focusing particularly upon "above the line" workers such as "producers, actors, directors, and writers," Rosten's study offers a rich portrait and critical analysis of Hollywood's internal social organization and culture. Similarly, anthropologist Hortense Powdermaker sought to better under-stand Hollywood's influence on individuals and American society by looking at the practices and beliefs of American film workers. Her book, *Hollywood: The Dream Factory* (1950) draws upon a year of fieldwork in Los Angeles that included interviews and observation to provide a rigorous ethnography and analysis of the social system organizing film production in Hollywood. Though Powdermaker is quick to suggest that Hollywood films are escapist fantasies, she crucially takes the norms, mores, and myths of Hollywood workers seriously, and provides a deep sense of how such beliefs influence industrial organization and practice and, in the end, movie content.

During this period, Harold Innis's work in the Canadian context marked another key intervention in our understanding of media and power by focusing attention on the historical study of technologies of communication. An economic historian by training, Innis's initial research on the history of trade in Canada (fur, fishing, and timber) led to a focus on the economic and political implications of transport and communication. As Scannell points out, Innis's discovery that the Canadian Pacific railroad "overlaid the routes of the old fur trade" marked the beginnings of his interest in how empires and nations manage and control vast territories, and the crucial role of communica-tions technologies in the exercise of imperial and national hegemony. In *Empire and Communication* (1950) and *The Bias of Communication* (1951), Innis offers a sweeping historical account of oral and literate cultures, the biases inherent in different technologies, and goes on to argue that space-biased media (more ephemeral media that spread widely at the time of creation but do not endure) were crucial to the consolidation of political power.

Broad claims aside, the significance of Innis's work for media industry studies lies in his focus on the material and political dimensions of media and communication technologies. Innis's work encourages us first and foremost to consider how media are recorded, stored, and circulated, and then to ponder the link between these processes and state and corporate power. It is not surprising that this line of thinking, one that brings together economic history, politics, and cultural geography, inspired theory building in the 1970s that began analyzing the ways in which Western dominance of the production and circulation of media shored up new forms of hegemony and the rise of American empire in the post-World War II era.

An influential body of scholarship began highlighting the fact that a large number of developing nations had to import news and entertainment programs from the developed West and, in the process, also imported powerful representations and values of capitalist consumer culture. Analysis by Herbert Schiller (1969), Armand Mattelart and Ariel Dorfman (1975), Oliver Boyd-Barrett (1977), Dallas Smythe (1977; 1981), and others directed a line of critique not only at the tradition of "administrative" research in mass communication-oriented departments across the United States but also toward "development communication," an influential area of research that focused attention on links between media and national development. The idea of development was straightforward – media could be used as vehicles for moving newly independent countries across the Global South toward the free market-oriented political economic model of the developed West. However, this perspective set up Western standards as an uncritiqued ideal.

While theories of dependency and cultural imperialism gained ground, the work of Latin-American scholars proved crucial for resisting the influence of the decidedly Anglocentric development communication framework. Using a neo-Marxist perspective that foregrounded capitalism and structural inequality as starting points for understanding international communications, Mattelart (1976) and others argued that transnational corporations based in the Global North brought the economies of postcolonial nations into a web of inter-dependency. The economic and geopolitical relations set in place had led to a highly exploitative dependency model that ensured the dominance of the Western "core" and left "peripheral" countries on the margins of the global economy. Latin American scholars took the lead in developing this body of scholarship and emphasized that media companies based in the Anglophone West were, in fact, the beneficiaries of "development" and "modernization" projects, and that creating new markets for their products across South America, Africa, and Asia was, in the end, the main goal. We delve into the complexities of this phase of media and communications research in greater detail later in this book, but for now, let us simply note that research on the media industries – newspaper and radio in particular – was central to fierce scholarly and public debates on the role of media, information, and communications in the emerging post-World War II world order.

The developments chronicled thus far are arguably categorized as a pre-history to the expansive and pluriform explosion of media industry study that emerges from the socio-political events and conditions at the end of the 1960s. Also of note during this period, structuralism and semiology increasingly dominated scholarship about film and media, which provided a method to study the ways in which media texts create meaning. Importantly, structuralism provided an alternative to the more impressionistic forms of "film appreciation" or auteur theory by attempting to study film and media with scientific rigor. Film studies rarely considered the industrialized mechanics of its production, while questions of "film form" gave way to analyses of film as a "language," with discernable properties and organizing principles. Scholars working within these textual traditions maintained an interest in media power, but located that power within discourse, form, and language and less within the institutions that make media.

From the Cauldron of the Late 1960s

While the period around 1968 is widely remembered as a significant inflection point and moment of social change in many parts of the globe, the importance of this period for establishing multiple trajectories of media *industry* study is less well known. The social and political upheaval of the time led many in search of ways to understand the operation of power in society, and the role of communication and media in that operation. Multiple structures for understanding the role of media industries emerged, although, instead of recognizing the common interests that could unite them, for the most part, these intellectual trajectories coexisted with little exchange, and in some cases, interactions were hostile when exchange occurred.

The social and political unrest of the late 1960s provided the seed that generated the three trajectories of thought that prepared the emergence of a coherent media industry studies in the early 2000s: critical political economy, cultural studies, and new historicism in film studies. Notably, all of these research traditions emerge out of a larger ferment involving the re-framing of Marxism but otherwise chart markedly different courses.

Critical Political Economy Approaches

Critical political economy approaches to the study of media and communication developed from a belief that control of media systems was a
vital part of how institutions and ideologies sustain their power. Much of
the research into this approach focuses on understanding how political
and economic power in societies is maintained by examining the use of
technological and institutional communication infrastructures.

Questions of empire, in particular, American imperialism in relation
to the role of media in national development in the mid 1960s, were a
key initial driver of critical political economy's approach to examining
the role of media systems in maintaining structures of power. These
concerns led to the set of recommendations produced by UNESCO
to improve global media known as the New World Information and
Communication Order (NWICO) in the 1970s. The broader context of
concern developed following the wave of decolonization in the 1950s
and 1960s and the ensuing struggles faced by postcolonial nations to set
up, or, in some cases, reform, their media industries. Critical political
economy analysis addressed many of the central problems of media
operation, including the narrow and rare attention to what were then
conceived of as "Third World" contexts in Western media and the
challenges these countries faced in developing their own media institutions. While there were clear material developmental concerns and
cultural implications of content issues, such as minimal and disaster-
focused news coverage, critical political economy and understanding
of the commercial and public funding structures helped explain these
content patterns. This strand of analysis is connected intimately to the
"dependency theory" that develops out of the Latin American context
(Mattelart and Dorfman, 1975) and remains strong well into the early
1980s.

Critical political economy also could account for the "west to
rest" pattern of media flow that drew concern about the advancement
of Western hegemony and stymying of indigenous production. Such
patterns arose from industrial structures such as the large and relatively
affluent US domestic market that enabled the selling of US media goods
around the globe at costs far less than those incurred in the original
production (Schiller, 1969).

This research into global empire and inequity in media, which focuses
on a macro level of research and investigates international flows of
capital and politics, is characteristic of the level of analysis explored in
Chapter 6. Critical political economy approaches often focus on this
macro scale, but were also used to investigate the practices and dynamics
within particular media institutions in the 1970s. A critical political

economy approach provides a key foundation for research characteristic of other levels, especially the organizational level considered in
Chapter 4. Much of this scholarship emerges from sociologists who
take methodologies of observation and interview into media organizations – primarily those producing news in the UK and US – to answer
questions about how and why the news comes to take its typical form.
A body of scholarship about newsroom organizations emerged in
parallel from sociologists, who examined media entities as organizations, though not always with the same Marxist underpinnings (Gans,
1979; Hirsch, 1972; Peterson, 1982). Whether it was Herbert Gans,
who examined US newsmaking at CBS, NBC, *Newsweek* and *Time*, or
Philip Schlesinger (1978), who investigated the newsmaking process in
the BBC, this branch of scholarship investigated how power operates
within newsrooms as organizations by considering issues such as the
practices that incentivize journalists toward a set of behaviors and the
routines that likewise structure newsgathering and reporting. As Stephen
Reese (2009) argues: "This approach moves away from treating news as
a question of bias and embeds it in the ongoing activities of organizations" (280). In contrast to assumptions that simplistically afforded the
publisher the power to decide what is news, this tradition explored the
inner workings of the organizations, their structures of power, and daily
routines, in order to develop far more sophisticated understandings of
how journalists are acculturated and how they perpetuate power structures through common practices. Hesmondhalgh offers a deeper insight
into the intellectual history of British versus North American political
economy traditions (2019), as well as explores differing approaches
within sociology (2009).

The BBC became a key target of study due to its perceived influence
in constructing understandings of contentious cultural debates of the
time, and this inspired the formation of scholarly collectives such
as the Glasgow University Media Group, Birmingham's Centre for
Contemporary Cultural Studies, and one at the University of Westminster,
which focused on exploring issues of how newsrooms decide what to
cover and how to cover it in great depth (Schlesinger, 1978; Burns, 1977;
Tuchman, 1978; Gans, 1979; Glasgow Media Group, 1976). Notably,
not all of the research focused on news organizations. Documentary
(Elliott, 1972) and scripted television series also were investigated in the
UK (Alvarado and Buscombe, 1978), and prime-time entertainment is
the focus of Todd Gitlin's (1983) expansive account of the US television
industry in the early 1980s. These studies of operations within organizations and the industrial practices characteristic of making media
provided a different layer of insight than was available from the analysis
of macro data about ownership, revenue, and media flows. Such studies

THE ORIGINS OF MEDIA INDUSTRY STUDIES 19

explored how power – whether to achieve profit or advance political goals – operates within media organizations and structures the choices available to those working within them.

Many of the British scholars then using a critical political economy of communication approach had experience of the student protests of the 1960s, and had begun their careers working in media (Murdock and Golding, 1973; Garnham, 1979). Notably, this strand of British research takes shape as the Polytechnic of Central London (predecessor to Westminster) began offering Britain's first media studies degree in 1975. As James Curran (2004) recounts, most of the Westminster "pioneers" had studied English literature at university, and they were all deeply affected by student protests, second-wave feminism, and other social issues brought to prominence during the late 1960s and early 1970s. Scholars at Westminster took, in Curran's formulation, the "materialist low road" and focused on the history and political economy of the media, the development of media institutions, issues of technological change, and policy and regulation. Curran also points out that Westminster staff's involvement in the media sector – Garnham at BBC2, Vincent Porter's documentary experience, Colin Sparks and Curran's involvement with political journalism, and so on – likely meant that they were "acutely aware of the importance of resource allocation and institutional processes" in the making of programs (16). Paddy Scannell and David Cardiff's (1991) primary research in the BBC archives was also crucial in that it alerted them to the importance of accounting for how a media program – a radio broadcast, for instance – is actually put together in a specific organization at a particular historical moment. Curran argues: "The Westminster tradition developed a strong interest in the 'political' aspect of the political economy tradition, marking a break from the narrow materialism represented by pioneers like Dallas Smythe" (21).

This research, focused on media organizations within critical political economy, is much less developed among North American scholars, who maintain focus on more macro structures that require different methodologies. The term critical political economy within North America is most closely associated with scholars influenced by the thinking of Adorno, Innis, and Smythe and arguably took a stronger Marxist approach and gave less consideration to culture than had Innis (Babe, 2009). In the United States, generations trained by Smythe and Schiller maintained a focus on broad, but generalized relationships of power. Vincent Mosco (2009) recounts a meeting in Illinois in 1979 as a key event in the development of North American political economy, that included Thomas Guback, Janet Wasko, Eileen Meehan, Oscar Gandy, and began the construction of the Union for Democratic Communications (88).

Notably, the work of these scholars focused on the film and broadcasting industries (Guback, 1969; Wasko, 1982; Meehan, 1983).

Research characteristic of critical political economy approaches was motivated in order to identify how communication and media industries reproduce power in response to the brash and stark global evidence of media power in postcolonial states, Cold War struggles, and the identity politics that grew increasingly contentious in Western nations. Such an approach at times focused on state policies and, at others, the daily practices of making news. Notably, many of these same concerns animated the exploration of media industries that simultaneously developed among cultural studies researchers and in the new history of film scholars.

Cultural Studies

Another major precursor to contemporary media industry studies is "cultural studies," which first emerges in England in the 1950s and 1960s as an endeavor on the part of leftist humanists to understand "culture," broadly conceived, in relation to working-class people and experiences. Although "cultural studies" has come to be applied to many different approaches, we focus on its critical and materialist version. This project became formally institutionalized with the formation of the Birmingham Centre for Contemporary Cultural Studies (CCCS) in 1964, although related work would appear in other locations into the 1970s. Importantly, cultural studies upheld that "culture" did not exclusively entail the fine arts or "high" culture but rather that it included everyday, lived practices and experiences; in this way, cultural studies opened a crucial path for the study of film, television, and other popular forms of media. Moreover, cultural studies emerged out of a generational shift in Marxist thinking and pushed scholars to understand culture as the product of material and social activities. As Nick Couldry notes (2015, 2), Raymond Williams advocated that we move "beyond Marx's crude distinction between 'base' and 'superstructure' and develop a 'notion of cultural production'" (1979, 139). In his famous "Cultural Studies: Two Paradigms" essay, Stuart Hall likewise argued that language needed to be regarded as a material process within what he called "a properly materialist theory of culture" (1980a, 72). In other words, Hall advanced a theory that attends fully to concrete material conditions and practices as well as to issues of social organization, structure, and ideology.

When Hall became the director of CCCS in 1969 – an institution also inspired by the events of May 1968 – his and much other work in cultural studies focused concertedly on the media and ideology.

Journal, Spring 1979), scholarly monographs and collections devoted to industrial aspects of cinema began to be more regularly published in the 1980s. Much of this work developed as part of a broader "historical turn" within film studies, which was driven more by empirical research than theoretical speculation. Such work complicated received histories of early cinema by clarifying the historical record through archival research, by arguing for the complexity and importance of films from this era, and by situating cinema within industrial and social contexts (e.g. Abel, 1987; Allen, 1980; Gunning, 1986; Musser, 1990).

A number of studies of "Classic Hollywood" emerged in the 1980s that added new insight and attention to early Hollywood's industrial operation. Perhaps the most notable of these is David Bordwell, Janet Staiger, and Kristin Thompson's *The Classical Hollywood Cinema: Film Style and Mode of Production to 1960* (1985), which explicitly connects textual features to industrial conditions and shifts the lens from examining film texts to exploring the entire industrial infrastructure, not simply the role of the camera. The "mode of production" component of the book was emphasized by Staiger, who traces her attention to industrial factors to many influences, including being the daughter of a newspaper print setter, as well as graduate training by Douglas Gomery. Gomery earned an MA in economics at the University of Wisconsin-Madison in 1970, before completing a PhD in Communication Arts in 1975. He produced extensive early models of media industry scholarship. His dissertation research explored the arrival of new technology – sound – in the American film industry, and he authored books and articles on the changing business of film exhibition, media ownership, and the studio system; he is well known as the co-author, with Robert Allen, of *Film History: Theory and Practice,* published the same year as the *Classical Hollywood Cinema.*

In this text, Allen and Gomery establish four types of film history: aesthetic, technological, economic, and social. This subcategorization of economic history creates an identifiable subarea that develops into a foundational strand of media industry studies. Some work along these lines continued through the 1990s, such as with Justin Wyatt's study of "high concept" cinema (1994). Though identified at the time as a kind of "film history," Gomery, Staiger, Tom Schatz, and Tino Balio crafted histories that illuminate the industrial processes of the film industry and trained a generation of students who took these methods and this approach beyond the bounds of film. One of the major contributions of film studies to media industry studies more generally is consequently to demonstrate the importance of historical work and industrial historiography, built upon extensive archival research and analysis of primary documents.

The three main intellectual approaches that allowed something identifiable as "media industry studies" to take shape in the early twenty-first century were profoundly influenced by a search for tools and ideas that could explain different aspects of the relationship between culture and politics during the late 1960s. Those working within both cultural studies and political economy conversations were interested in media power and understood industry as a site of power, but focused on examining that power in different places and believed it to operate in subtly different ways. Broadly speaking, this phase of political economy research attends minimally to actual media content, whereas the cultural studies scholars emerging out of the CCCS sought to understand how news organizations *framed* events and communities based on content they observed (*Policing the Crisis*). It can be argued that the operation of power was less central to the historical industrial studies emerging within film studies but, crucially, much of the film scholarship sought to connect the composition of films with the industrial practices of their creation.

In addition to establishing three disparate approaches, the study of particular media tended to be divided among these traditions. Though scholars such as Thomas Guback (1969) and Janet Wasko (1982) examined cinema from a critical political economic perspective, this approach otherwise largely focused on the study of news and journalism. Cultural studies also considered news – as *Policing the Crisis* (Hall et al., 1978) and the *Nationwide* studies (Brunsdon and Morley, 1978; Morley, 1980) illustrate – but operated with a more expansive sense of cultural influence that encouraged study of the institutions behind "softer" news, such as *Panorama*, as well as a breadth of media and popular culture forms, and became influential for taking such forms of culture seriously. The strand of industry study developing in film studies unsurprisingly focused on film – although, by the mid 1980s, the emerging generation of scholars blended cultural studies with film history to also develop robust studies of television. Perhaps this segregation of object of study accounts for the limited cross-pollination among these related conversations at this time.

This account condenses a broad literature and focuses heavily on key works produced in the US and UK, when there were often significant divergences in the core practices and foci between these two national contexts. Of course, related inquiry also developed elsewhere and was often in conversation, but also offered contrasting political, economic, and industrial histories. For example, what we describe as distinct trajectories of political economy, cultural studies, and film studies were far more intertwined in Australian media scholarship (Turner, 1990; Cunningham and Turner, 1993) than the discrete histories presented here suggest. Political economy, cultural studies, and film studies may have drawn common inspiration from postcolonial conditions and late 1960s' cultural unrest, but distinctions in disciplinary placement and object of study often prevented significant conversations across these areas until the 1980s.

Media Go Global in the Late 1980s: Reassessing Cultural Studies and Critical Political Economy

Roughly two decades after the social, political, and industrial forces which inspired the examination of media industries that began in the late 1960s, a similar combination of these forces, as well as techno-logical change, again drew attention to media industries. Beginning in the mid-1980s, a number of nation-states across Asia, Africa, and Latin America adopted a series of market-oriented policies that were designed to integrate their economies into a global system of trade and commerce. Under immense political and economic pressure from the West, several countries sought to reduce the role and size of the state in the economy. A number of countries dismantled state monopolies, reduced tariffs and taxes, and invited foreign investment in a number of sectors including media and telecommunications. By the mid-1990s, these structural changes led to dramatic expansion in the media indus-tries and rapid privatization and corporatization of film, television, advertising, and, at the time, a nascent ICT sector (Chakravartty and Zhao, 2008). These changes were most noticeable in the audiovisual industries, where VCRs and satellite communication expanded the range of films and television programs available, enabled the growth of trans-national media, and introduced commercial competitors into countries long dominated by public service or government-funded regimes. The entry of foreign players also sparked local competition, with a host of regional and national media firms challenging the reach of transnational media companies. On the whole, top-down theories of core-periphery flows of communication that accounted for Cold War structures, as well as neo-colonial relations of dependency, no longer held the same explanatory power.

Schiller (1992) himself updated his work to acknowledge that the geopolitical structures of the 1960s and 1970s had shifted in dramatic ways, but underscored the importance of focusing on new forms of American cultural domination. Other scholars, particularly those who had delved into film studies' and cultural studies' approaches to media and communication, began advocating a more nuanced understanding of the links between political-economic power, on the one hand, and media and cultural power on the other. While audience studies made it clear that viewers in varied social contexts are not cultural dupes who adopt, in a straightforward fashion, consumerist and capitalist values "encoded" in films and television programs, an emergent body of scholarship on the localization of cable and satellite television (Parks and Kumar, 2002; Kraidy, 2005), the complex ways in which state-run media organizations were reconfiguring their operations in the face of new competition (Kumar, 2006; Straubhaar, 1991), and inter-regional flows that at times bypassed American media almost entirely (Iwabuchi, 2010) made it clear that sweeping claims about media industries across the Global South being under the thrall of Western media corporations did not hold up well under closer scrutiny.

By the early 1990s, when the multi-polar media world with which we are familiar today was beginning to take shape, David Morley and Kevin Robins argued that a "social theory that is informed by the geographical imagination" (1995, 6) was crucial to understanding changes in media and communication. Surveying the political and economic transformations that had transformed national economies across the world since the late 1970s, they focused in particular on the increasingly complex spatial relations that the mobility of capital had engendered as the "essential context for understanding the nature and significance of developments in the media industries." Put simply, it was becoming clear that media scholars needed to look not only beyond Western nations and issues of media imperialism, but also had to re-examine the assumption that media industries functioned largely within the boundaries established by nation-states. Nation-states did matter, but the 'national' was not necessarily *the* dominant scale at which the globalization of media industries was playing out.

For instance, the spatial coordinates and geographic reach of a major industry like Bollywood had changed dramatically over the course of the 1990s. The answer to the question: "Where in the world is Bollywood?" was, to be sure, "Mumbai." However, Mumbai's emergence as a global media capital could no longer be grasped without mapping the city's links with other centers of finance, technology, the South Asian diaspora, and creative work such as New York, Los Angeles, and London, among others. And the same claim could be made of the Chinese film and TV industries, the ICT sector in Ghana, and certainly of Hollywood. Further, it was neither possible nor productive to conceptualize Bollywood as a film industry. Television and digital media had emerged as central to the circulation of Bollywood content across the world, in expanding and redefining sites and modes of consumption, and enabling filmmakers and stars to envision overseas markets and audiences. Such shifts in social, economic, and technological conditions required newer approaches to global media industries than those rooted in theories of development, dependency, and cultural imperialism.

Film studies also took its heightened attention to industry to other national contexts. Within film studies, there was a tradition of Western scholars studying the cinemas of particular countries, which typically engaged in textual analyses and claims regarding films' national character, and which might make some reference to industrial issues (Kracauer, 1947; Anderson and Richie, 1959; Richie, 1971). Yet, the study of different nations' cinemas with an interest in the *idea* of "national cinema" truly appeared in the 1980s, and continued strongly through the 1990s, as a distinct strain within film studies that, importantly, sometimes included discussions of these countries' film industries. Such work included accounts that were variously descriptive, detailed, and analytical of industrial history, within broader accounts of a nation's cinema (Armes, 1987; Elsaesser, 1989; Hayward, 1993; Street, 1997). Although industry was not the main concern of this "national cinemas" scholarship, this work was important for distinguishing the features of different film industries, typically with the aim of helping to explain how and why stylistic or generic trends occurred. Much of this industrial analysis within national cinemas' scholarship takes a broad view of industrial structures, policies, and practices. Further, this work is guided by the fact that a number of cases entail direct state support for a cinema industry (France, Germany, etc.), which not only distinguishes these cinemas from Hollywood but, perhaps obviously, makes these industries politically "national" in a direct manner. Anne Jäckel's study of European film industries (2003) is to be distinguished in this regard, as it focuses directly on industrial structures and national and *multi-national* policy instruments used to facilitate domestic and pan-European cinematic production in the face of increasing globalization.

Research using a critical political economy approach certainly attended to the shifting patterns of media globalization, but another significant focus through the 1990s was the considerable consolidation of media industries (from many competitors to few) and conglomeration (from single industry players to multi-industry holdings). A lot of this scholarship provided descriptive accounts (Bagdikian, 2004) of the steadily diminishing number of owners as mergers and acquisitions spread from within a single industry sector, while others analyzed regulatory shifts that enabled the massive deals of the 1990s that conglomerated the industry (Holt, 2011). In the midst of these changes, Wasko (1994) examined continuities and changes in the broadly conceived "entertainment industry" brought about by new technologies, such as cable and home video. The scholarship was consistently critical, and often polemical, predicting that conglomeration would result in homogenization of cultural goods (McChesney, 1997). In contrast, economist Benjamin Compaine (1979; Compaine and Gomery, 2000) applied a wider range of economic principles and developed richly contextualized accounts of the many forces at play, industry by industry, to offer a more nuanced account of shifting ownership norms in the United States. In practice, it was too early to identify clear results, as the scale of integration by these companies required a decade of restructuring. The true repercussions of the consolidation and conglomeration were arguably overlooked a decade later, as the anticipated and real implications of "the internet" became a focus, just as the new conglomerates established their reconfiguration.

Television Studies Incorporates Industry

Separate from the political, regulatory, and technological forces that had begun to substantially adjust the operation of many media industries and inspire new approaches and lines of inquiry, the cultural studies approach to the study of media industries was being refigured by growing conversation between cultural studies and the new film history. Film scholars – particularly those training in film programs in the 1980s and 1990s – began investigating popular culture more broadly, especially television, and considered industrial questions in their studies. By the early 1990s, a wave of books integrated cultural studies' circuit of culture models that included production with film history's investigation of how modes of production affect textual outcomes, and these books became a foundation for television studies in the United States (Anderson, 1994; Balio, 1990; Boddy, 1993; Caldwell, 1995; Curtin, 1995; D'Acci, 1994; Hilmes, 1990; Spigel, 1992). Most of these works used archival research to develop rich, evidence-based understandings of dynamics of regulation and industrial practice, particularly of the early years of US television. Importantly, many of these authors began training graduate students in the 1990s and introduced industry study as a crucial component of media studies scholarship.

What might have been a much earlier arrival of a coherent media industry studies in the early 1990s was derailed by vehement disagreements among some critical political economists and cultural studies scholars in the early 1990s (Babe, 2009). Admittedly, the question of industry study and the role of media industries in media power was never engaged in this debate (see Colloquy, 1995), which centered on strawman constructions of both approaches. Through the late 1990s, cultural studies and political economy were seen as incompatible in North America, at least among those studying audiovisual media. Though this debate delayed conversations, it may have encouraged the coherence of a media industry studies later.

Industrial studies of popular music and journalism weren't part of these debates, and existed as an organic part of separate intellectual journal and conference communities built around these media forms. Of course, there are also many other important influences that did not clearly align with the approaches of political economy, cultural studies, or film history. Media economics rarely considered culture with much complexity, but this scholarship helped inform more complicated accounts of industrial operations (Compaine, 1979; Owen and Wildman, 1992; Picard, 2002). Also, various forms of organizational study and sociological study of media entities as organizations produced insights valuable for media industry studies, even if their central concerns and questions were different (Hirsch, 1972; Peterson, 1982). Most notably, Joseph Turow's (1992) exploration of organizational dynamics and pressures in media industries provided an early framework for understanding the diverse array of roles and the negotiations among them that are part of broad production and circulation processes.

Conclusion

We offer the start of an intellectual lineage for media industry studies, one that needs to be expanded beyond its US/UK and audiovisual biases. Still, we can discern patterns and some degree of coherence. It is notable that scholars turn to questions of how media are made and circulated at some of the most disruptive political and cultural junctures of the last century. Our account of the significance of the late 1960s' unrest in some of these intellectual histories draws from interviews and accounts of those who were part of creating these disparate thought-collectives, and their reflection on the development – and growing coherence – of some scholarly conversations over the intervening years. Though this chapter merely scratches the surface of a rich literature, we hope to have created a bibliography that proves useful for those entering the field and looking to situate themselves in relation to multiple and overlapping intellectual communities.

We conclude this account with the close of the twentieth century and take up accounts of the years since in the book's conclusion, where we address the key topics of new media and internet distribution, further globalization of media, and the conglomeration and consolidation of media ownership that figured prominently in the first decade of the twenty-first century. Chapter 2 now transitions to the primary organization of the book around levels or scales of industry study, beginning with the micro level of individuals and particular roles, and working up to examinations of how political structures negotiated among nation-states and global economics also explain how media industries produce and circulate cultural forms in historically and geographically contextualized ways.

2

Individuals and Roles

When we think about the media, we often think about the films and television programs we like, the radio shows and podcasts we listen to, the stars we adore, the apps we use, and the games we play. And when we are asked to think about the industries that produce and circulate the media that so profoundly shape our lives and worlds, we often think about larger-than-life individuals who wield enormous influence. Mark Zuckerberg or Oprah Winfrey need no introduction in the Western hemisphere and neither do Jack Ma in Asia or Walid Al Ibrahim across the Middle East and North Africa region. Indeed, public debates about the workings of the media industries – particularly in terms of business, policy, and regulation – often focus attention on founders, CEOs, and other powerful moguls at the helm of large and powerful companies and conglomerates like News Corp., Amazon, Apple, Disney, Alibaba, and so on. This emphasis on key individuals shapes our view of the creative side of the media industries as well. The names and personas of major film directors, television producers, and game designers are part and parcel of regular news coverage and our knowledge of the media industries.

But we rarely hear stories about the numerous other individuals whose daily routine and careful work sustains the production, circulation, and maintenance of various media forms. Graphic designers in newsrooms, talent scouts in the music industry, casting agents for film and television, content moderators working for social media platforms, and many others play incredibly key roles. Media scholars, however, have tended to underplay the influence of individuals, focusing instead on the broader organizational and political-economic structures within which individuals are situated. When we have focused on individuals within the media industries, the story has tended to revolve around ideas of creative genius (film directors as auteurs or a famous news broadcaster as an agent of political change). The reality, as often the case, is more complicated and requires contextualization.

An emergent body of scholarship in media industry studies focuses precisely on this terrain – the particular roles and individuals involved in industrialized media production. Wide-ranging studies on this domain of the media industries tend to focus on specific jobs in the media and pose questions that broaden our understanding of the contribution of particular roles to the complicated industrialized fields that are characteristic of the production and circulation of media commodities. Studies at this level do often examine specific personas – a film studio mogul, an esteemed director, a remarkable editor, or notable music producer. The subjects of such studies are quite often exceptional individuals whose public personas have been carefully crafted over many years, if not decades. A closer look at their trajectories within the media industries reveals their singular influence, but also maps the broader economic, political, and socio-cultural dynamics that both enable and curtail their agency.

In other words, the complex, specialized, and multifaceted processes of production and circulation place significant limits on individuals. Individuals always contend with broader structures of management and typically only affect a small part of the complex process spanning idea generation to a completed media product reaching an audience. But hundreds of singular actions and choices by individuals account for the media goods produced and the paths by which they reach audiences. For instance, a director may make the final decision on many facets of a film, but those who report to the director significantly narrow the range of options that are considered across the full range of production, and thus exert agency in narrowing the options suggested.

The individual is always a part of the whole, possessing what Timothy Havens and Amanda Lotz describe as "circumscribed agency" (2014), drawing upon theories of power and agency developed by Michel Foucault (1979) and Antonio Gramsci (1971). Indeed, industry scholars mobilize a wide range of theories of social and cultural power as they contend with the role that different individuals play within the greater media industries. For example, elsewhere Havens (2014) adopts Anthony Giddens's theory of "structuration" (1984) as a way of analyzing the dialectic of agency and structure that shapes media workers' power. Others draw from the sociological analysis of Pierre Bourdieu (1984) to examine various media workers as "intermediaries" that influence the social meanings of media products as they are produced and circulated (du Gay et al., 1997; du Gay, 1997; Negus, 1999). In these works and others, it is clear that studying individuals and professional roles often *requires* an analysis of power, agency, and influence.

Studies of media industry roles and the individuals who perform them examine how different tasks of production and circulation are organized, assigned, and performed, and with what consequence. To some degree, the actions of individuals are evident throughout the other levels we explore in this book, but the individual or the practices involved in a particular role are often obscured or aggregated in such a way as to allow the operational norms and practices of industries, organizations, or productions to take priority. Of course, conglomerates, industries, organizations, and productions are structures composed of individuals, but focusing on individuals and particular roles adds another layer of insight to our understanding of the operation of media industries. An expansive range of questions can drive research primarily organized at the level of roles or individuals. But as we will see in the research examples explored in this chapter, it is vital to move beyond descriptive case studies and connect specific individuals and/or roles to larger questions and concerns in media industry studies writ large.

This chapter highlights the broad range of media industries research that has sought to develop richer understandings of the roles individuals can play, how they negotiate various constraints within and beyond the media industries, and the ramifications of these negotiations. Drawing on studies focused on individuals and roles in a range of industries, we point to assumptions and conditions so deeply entrenched that they persist across industries. We also address instances in which taken for granted norms can appear strange, especially during moments of technological, political, and cultural flux. In some studies, issues related to labor conditions loom large. Others build accounts that offer something like a supply chain analysis as they focus on the additive contribution of the particular role in question.

The contribution of scholarship focused on individuals and roles is often two-fold. By shedding light on the everyday practices of media professionals and their roles in complex organizations, this vein of research helps scholars gain a more nuanced understanding of media industries, given that most of us typically have little experience with the day-to-day operation of media industries. More broadly, rich descriptions of seemingly mundane practices can provide a window into the tasks and the negotiation of agency available to those who produce and circulate cultural goods. Kyle Barnett's (2014) work on talent scouts in the US recording industry in the early twentieth century is a good example. Barnett describes how "record men" negotiated social and cultural divides (rural and urban taste cultures, for instance) that shaped the music industry's expansion and transformation at the time. On some level, this may seem a very particular inquiry, perhaps valuable only to those interested in the history of the recording industry in the United States. Indeed, the descriptive context of his study might only be so narrowly valuable, but in practice, Barnett provides something far more widely applicable.

Every media worker in every industry, at every place, and every time negotiates within macro forces and organizational norms, and nuanced research at this level aims to engage and advance an understanding of these dynamics. For Barnett, this meant exploring the fragmentation of music forms such as what we now call jazz, blues, and country within the United States and the contentious meanings and cultural politics connected to those forms at the time. Such moments of contestation arguably repeat regularly throughout the history of recorded music. The period Barnett explores is the boom time of industrial expansion of the phonograph as a result of expiring patents. Indeed, there is a long history of technological innovations being intimately linked to format changes and even the emergence of new media forms and genres. Many of the dilemmas raised by "new" technologies often can be explained by reflecting on earlier periods of disruption. Moreover, examining the role and practices of talent agents for recorded music might provide insights or help lay the foundation for theorizing about a wide range of cultural intermediaries across media industries, including, for instance, talent agents who manage "influencers" on social media platforms.

Barnett's article is by no means unique when it comes to well-constructed research on individuals or roles within media industries, but it offers a striking illustration of the need to approach research projects by reading broadly and engaging with broader conceptual issues and questions. Put simply, scholarship on individuals and their roles within a larger site of cultural production can and should generate new insights into the workings of the media industries at large.

This chapter begins with a brief discussion of scholarship on auteurs, or film directors that have been heralded within the industry and popular culture as especially creative or important. Although most auteur studies are *not* within the realm of media industry studies, the figure of the "auteur" is so commonly held up as an important figure in the film industry that we think it is helpful to point toward those auteur studies that *do* engage in industrial analysis. Looking at an auteur might well provide insights into the greater movie business. The chapter proceeds with a discussion of a wide range of other figures who play important roles in producing different media, such as writers, music supervisors, and video-game developers. Part of our objective here is to highlight the complex arrangement of labor and resources that media production requires.

But of course, the making of media constitutes only one element of any given industry and, accordingly, this chapter moves on to a discussion of media workers who enable the distribution and circulation of media products. Our examples include attention to the role that video clerks play in the circulation of media on a local level, the roles of diasporic media entrepreneurs who facilitate the flow of media in transnational circuits, and the emergence of software developers of algorithmic recommender systems that have reconfigured media circulation in our current digital age. Finally, because scholarship that focuses on individuals and professional roles might risk offering a fragmented or partial portrait of any given industry, this chapter closes with an examination of talent agents who help connect different aspects of the movie business. In looking at two studies that differ significantly in research materials and methods, we see the crucial role played by talent agents and agencies historically and more recently. The comparison and contrast of these studies also allows us to consider deeper questions about how scholars study individuals.

The Director, the Auteur

It has been a longstanding convention within film scholarship to research and write about the director. Indeed, it would be difficult to calculate the number of publications that examine some directors; studies of Alfred Hitchcock, for example, constitute a mini-industry of their own. The focus on directors derives from the presumption that they hold a privileged place of power and control over a film's production. However, most of this work does not necessarily contribute to "media industry studies" due to the dominance of "auteurism," or the notion that certain directors exert notable *creative* control over their films as "authors," an idea initiated by French film critics in the 1950s and popularized in the United States by Andrew Sarris in the 1960s. Auteurism prompted scholars to attend more to issues of textual form, style, and "personality" rather than work practices, labor conditions, or industrial contexts.

Indeed, much auteurist scholarship sought to single out the individual style of a director in spite of industrial context, without examining that context in any meaningful way. In fact, a number of industrial studies of classic Hollywood aimed to counter the idea that the director held a place of creative privilege within the industry (Schatz, 1988; Bordwell, Staiger, and Thompson, 1985). Relatedly, scholars have written about the power of the producer and the showrunner, and not the director, within the television industry (Newcomb and Alley, 1983). More recently, John Thornton Caldwell (2008) has shown how "negotiated and collective authorship is almost an unavoidable determining reality in contemporary film/television" (199).

Nevertheless, there are some directorial studies that attend to issues of industry dynamics and illustrate a director's industrial significance in a manner that could be described as "industrial auteurism" (Tzioumakis, 2006). Such work deviates from classical auteurism by studying directors not in terms of film form, but rather examines film authorship "in relation to economic, industrial, and institutional determinants" (Dombrowski, 2008, 2). Works along these lines include Justin Wyatt's article on Robert Altman (1996), Lisa Dombrowski's monograph about Samuel Fuller (2008), or Mark Gallagher's study of Steven Soderbergh (2014).

Some works of industrial auteurism treat auteurs as "extratextual" agents (Tzioumakis, 2006, 60) and examine discourses about a director in order to situate that director within a larger industrial context. In this vein, Jon Lewis's 1997 study of Francis Ford Coppola, *Whom God Wishes to Destroy ...*, approaches auteurism as a discursive category that Coppola himself used self-consciously as a form of industrial and promotional identity. "Coppola," he argues, "understood that he had to promote himself as an *auteur* ... in order to maintain a strong position within Hollywood" (19). The book details Coppola's efforts from the late 1970s through the early 1990s to gain industrial independence from Hollywood, due to his belief that the economic goals and managerial oversight of the Hollywood studios stifled creative filmmaking. This is made especially evident with Coppola's formation of Zoetrope Studios, which was intended as an independent studio that would produce and release films outside the Hollywood studio system. Lewis draws largely upon trade publications to build evidence of this narrative but, crucially, treats this material critically as "rumour" and "hype" that nevertheless serves important industrial functions of turf marking, agenda setting, and position taking. Lewis uses discourses coming out of trade press to construct a narrative regarding Coppola's industrial activities and motivations. In this way, Lewis's work shows how media industry studies can, at times, require more discursive than economic analysis, as industry scholars construct stories about industry and industrial workers.

Lewis covers the production and reception of Coppola's films during this period and describes Coppola's attempts to innovate film production work routines. He contextualizes these accounts with analysis of larger phenomena within the movie business at the time, such as changes in the ownership of different studios as well as the rise of home video. Looking at such macro-level phenomena enables Lewis to argue that

Coppola's decline in critical and industrial stature in the 1980s did not result entirely from him being a bad director or businessman, but rather from the director's inability to adapt to the changing conditions of the American movie industry in the 1980s.

Lewis's book thus contrasts with many auteurist studies by showing how this director's career reflected the condition of the Hollywood industrial system in the 1980s in a way that expands our understanding of the industry as a whole. It shows simultaneously how narratives regarding individual industrial workers are actively constructed, and how prominent figures, like auteurs, work within and reflect larger institutional and industrial contexts.

[JON LEWIS'S 1997 STUDY OF FRANCIS FORD COPPOLA]

Individuals Making Media

In contrast to studies of auteurs and other prominent individuals, recent work in media industry studies has opened the door to exploring a wider range of industry roles with varying goals and mandates. At the broadest level, research devoted to understanding the scope of a particular role involves grappling with a fundamental tension confronting media workers – how to contend with the opportunities for exerting one's agency, while negotiating the limits that are often a function of the high degree of specialization characteristic of media industry work.

In some cases, people in a particular role serve as informants for much more specific questions, as in the case of Alfred Martin's research about writers in the US media scene (2015). In fact, in addition to looking at directors and producers as important creative figures, a number of scholars have examined the work routines and functions of scriptwriters, and often assess writers' relative power within film and television industries (Banks, 2015; Conor, 2014; Redvall, 2013). In Martin's case, his interview-based research illustrates a focused line of inquiry. Martin identifies writing practices among black sitcom writers and their experiences creating black, gay characters as a site for exploring how industrial practices affect media content. Martin identifies how even when the major barrier of bringing diversity into writer's rooms is overcome, the agency of writers who advocate for historically underrepresented and marginalized communities can be limited by production hierarchies.

In looking at media production, one finds that threads of similarity and difference in work, working conditions, and how one gets work connect multiple media industries. Casting agents play a key role in shaping labor practices in audiovisual industries and in deciding the faces and bodies of the characters in popular storytelling. Media industry researchers have explored different questions about the work of casting agents and their role in media production. Kristin Warner's research is driven by questions about the causes of the lack of racial diversity on US television and how "colorblind" casting practices do little to acknowledge the discrepancy of the black experience on screen. Warner's (2015) research, which blends interviews with casting agents, observation of casting practices, and textual analysis, helps her build an argument for why "colorblind" casting practices fail to produce sophisticated representations of black American life despite their counter-racist aims. Her research expands our understanding of how casting works, how the power that a casting agent might wield in that role is delimited, and more broadly reveals how media workers in this role mobilize ideas about race and racial difference.

Erin Hill (2014) explores a different angle in her research that examines why casting shifted from being a male-dominated field. Through interviews and other accounts of casting director labor, Hill identifies how feminized skills of emotional labor have come to be perceived as central to success in this role. Hill's research is helpful because many fields in media industries are highly gender segregated, and many seek strategies to help diversify ranks. The case of such a pronounced transition may offer insight into such strategies well beyond the context of casting practices.

Also looking at the field of important figures in audiovisual media production, Paul McDonald (2013) brings media industries to star studies in his book on Hollywood stardom. Notably, McDonald's work breaks with the prevalence of interview research common here. Particularly in chapters that present case studies of specific stars, such as Tom Hanks, Will Smith, and Julia Roberts, McDonald draws from a wide array of archival and industrial data to present a comprehensive look at the financial implications of stardom in Hollywood filmmaking. He builds an extensive profile of the projects, remuneration, and commercial success of stars such as Smith, and traces shifts in representation and published interviews with the star, their representation (agents/managers), and studio workers to connect discourse about the star with studio valuation and outcomes. McDonald uses industry-produced data, such as Motion Picture Association of America accounting of grosses, and adds detail by investigating budget documents made public due to legal proceedings, as well as extensive secondary sources and trade journalism that provide details about the complicated financial underpinnings of some of the highest paid talent in media production. McDonald illustrates how, even though "star" is certainly a culturally constructed status, it is one with meaningful implications for the performance of Hollywood film studios and the decisions they make about which films to make.

Media industry studies has tended to focus on key creative roles including those of writers, directors, producers, and performers, at the expense of other domains of work and labor that are central to media production. Tim Anderson (2013) offers a valuable corrective and examines the connections between the popular music and screen industries by focusing on music supervisors – the professionals responsible for selecting the music for films and television programs. In addition to exploring the nature of this work, Anderson's analysis focuses on the shifting status of music supervisors, who he notes were widely disregarded at the beginning of the twenty-first century, but rapidly improved in esteem as placing popular music in television programs and films became increasingly important exposure for artists, and the dynamics of all media industries adapted to internet distribution. Anderson suggests that we think of music supervisors as a type of "intermediary," which is a common way of framing the work of media workers who connect the roles within production and circulation. Anderson's analysis relies on an expansive use of trade press accounts of music supervisors, which he interprets in relation to shifting industry practices, particularly in television, that provide broader context for the growing importance of this role.

Illustrating a broad approach toward examining professional roles in the media industries, Casey O'Donnell's *Developer's Dilemma: The Secret World of Video Game Developers* (2014) offers a book-length ethnography of game development that spans a video game's pre-production to its release. Positioning itself within science and technology studies (STS), O'Donnell's book draws from four years of observation and interviews in game studios in the United States and India to provide an inside look at a portion of the game industry that is often hidden behind the more commonly recognized names of publishers and console manufacturers. Where media industries' research often glosses over method, O'Donnell provides commendable detail, including explanation for choices about fieldsite selection. O'Donnell's embeddedness allows him to observe work conditions in the video-game industry and, in doing so, contributes to scholarship, not only on a specific media industry, but more broadly on work cultures shaped by digital technologies and multi-national work teams. Indeed, many of the issues he discusses, such as offshore outsourcing and permanent crunch-time work conditions, have parallels in other media industries including digital visual effects. O'Donnell's account can simultaneously inform an audience of STS readers curious about conditions that enable and constrain creative collaborative work and provide insight on the role of game developers and the broader labor conditions they must negotiate.

There is rich body of research about a diverse array of individuals and professional roles that have critical functions within different media industries and sectors. Indeed, each of these cases shows that one can gain a deeper understanding of an entire industry, or an important issue facing that industry, by selecting one professional role within it. As media studies re-orients itself beyond the Anglophone West, this emphasis on individuals and roles also promises to make vital contributions to global media and cultural histories. Take Sangita Gopal's (2019) work on feminism, television, and gendered media work in 1980s India, for instance. Focusing on a decade marked by a phenomenal expansion in television infrastructure, the cultivation of female viewership, the shift toward a globalized consumer culture across urban India, and crucially, the varied impact of second-wave feminism, Gopal examines the influence that a small group of women filmmakers came to wield. Drawing on policy reports, trade press documents, news coverage, and films and television programs, Gopal's analysis centers on one particular filmmaker, Sai Paranjpe, as a way to delineate the challenges that women faced in a rapidly shifting media and cultural ecology. Carefully situating Paranjpe's work in relation to a fraught politics of identity and her refusal to make so-called "women's films," Gopal examines how the demand for television programming – as well as the emergence of video – created new opportunities compared to the established, and largely closed, worlds of cinema and print media. Tracing Paranjpe's career across media forms and industries – radio (plays), television documentaries, tele-serials, TV plays, and films – Gopal demonstrates how a focus on individual roles can, in fact, spiral outward to reveal the emergence and evolution of an entire media industry (state-run television, in this case) and, in turn, the potential for gendered media work.

Taken together, these cases illustrate the range of broader issues – whether labor conditions, reproduction of racial and gender ideologies, or how roles evolve in response to broader industrial dynamics – that research on individuals working in the creation of media and their roles can inform. Further, the diversity of the scholarship discussed here aligns with the wide range of different roles and individuals that make up the expansive and intricately organized world of media production. The cases of research cited here could be replaced with an assortment of work examining other roles in media making. This all points to an important fact, however, that media production entails a massive and complex arrangement of workers and resources – relying essentially on many types of work and workers.

Individuals, Intermediaries, and Media Circulation

Despite the importance of many people in the making of media, production constitutes only one segment of the media industries. In order to be read, viewed, heard, or otherwise consumed by audiences, media must necessarily move through the world to reach those audiences. Thus, the roles of media distribution and circulation provide another fundamental aspect of the industry. Numerous figures play important roles in serving this industrial function, and some recent scholarship examines individuals who shape media circulation. These intermediary figures often occupy unglamorous positions within the larger media industries, perhaps explaining why they have been overlooked.

In his cultural and industrial study of the American video store, Daniel Herbert (2014) asserts the importance of the role played by the video clerk in the film industry by facilitating the circulation of movies in local communities. Herbert draws from employee training manuals and interviews to define the clerk as performing "a social role that comes about through specific practices and interactions" (72). He details clerks' typical work routines, including maintaining the store space and engaging in rental transactions with customers. Yet, because customers frequently ask for movie recommendations, clerks also function as intermediaries of taste. Herbert argues that despite their seeming insignificance to the larger movie industry, video clerks have been crucial to both the business of movie distribution and to the cultivation of movie tastes as well. Herbert does not directly invoke the literature on cultural intermediaries, but his characterization of clerks as mediating both economic and cultural values through retail transactions contributes to our understanding of industrial and cultural intermediaries more broadly.

Herbert draws from interviews with clerks across the United States to address different contexts such as "specialty" video stores that prioritize niche movie content, in contrast with small-town video stores. Looking at specific case studies, Herbert describes these clerks – sometimes anonymously, sometimes by name – and quotes them liberally to give a sense of their work lives and their beliefs about themselves and their jobs. He writes that clerks at specialty stores are often cinephiles with a "sense of mission and faith that their stores are sites of alternative culture" (87). These clerks often have an extensive knowledge of movies and eclectic tastes, which influences the way in which they serve as intermediaries of movie taste. In contrast, interviews reveal that small-town clerks typically are not cinephiles with elaborate knowledge of cinema or distinctive tastes in movies. Instead, they, "make [movie] suggestions based on their knowledge of the rental history of the person before them and/or as a calculated synthesis of feedback they have received from other customers" (136). In this way, Herbert argues, small-town clerks "*embody* movie culture" in their towns because of their ongoing interactions with their clientele.

Whereas Herbert's study of video clerks discusses their importance to the "localization" of media, Courtney Brannon Donoghue examines the role of movie industry professionals who are crucial to global media flows. Her book, *Localising Hollywood* (2017), shows how global media flows are shaped by distinct local media industries, work cultures, and individual workers, contrasting strongly with the political economic approach taken in *Global Hollywood* (discussed in Chapter 6), which draws its evidence from newspapers, trade publications, industrial, and government reports. Brannon Donoghue shows how Hollywood has localized its products and also facilitated the production of local-language film and television in a range of locations around the world, including Brazil, England, Germany, and Spain. Her work illustrates the complex negotiation that takes place as Hollywood operates around the world, and she focuses on industrial workers and roles that engage in this negotiation.

Her work is built in part on trade publications and other public-facing information regarding the movie business. Yet, *Localising Hollywood* draws upon extensive fieldwork and interviews with numerous industry professionals from six different countries. This reliance upon first-hand observations and practitioner accounts grounds Brannon Donoghue's broader assertions with empirical, behind-the-scenes concreteness and detail. Although interviews can be good sources of information for many types of industrial study, Brannon Donoghue's use of and quotations from interviews bolster her assertions regarding these individuals' agency in shaping Hollywood's global business activities.

In her examination of the individuals who enable Hollywood to localize its business operations on an international scale, Brannon Donoghue specifically details the roles played by the "country manager," also known as the "managing director" (MD), and the "director of production" at different studios' production offices for different regions. As she describes, managing directors oversee a team of employees responsible for releasing English-language content in a given territory or market, while the director of production manages a studio's local-language productions, or LLPs. These LLPs are an important form of Hollywood's industrial and cultural localization, making the director of production an important cultural intermediary. Thus, while *Localising Hollywood* provides an expansive view of a widespread business practice, Brannon Donoghue manages this largely through her similarly widespread research into the workers that make the practice possible.

Aswin Punathambekar offers yet another study of individuals who have significantly shaped global media flows. He focuses on the role played by diasporic media entrepreneurs in shaping Bollywood's transnational circulation, who also facilitate American media companies' expanding commercial interest in South Asian American audiences. The study examines two highly publicized diasporic media initiatives – MTV-Desi, a television channel that sought to target South Asian American (Desi) youth, which only lasted eighteen months, and Saavn. com, a New York-based digital media company that emerged as a prominent aggregator and distributor of Bollywood content in North America. Punathambekar narrates stories about non-resident Indian and diasporic media professionals working in a space defined on the one hand by a rapidly changing American media system, and on the other hand by increasingly influential Indian media companies that succeeded in courting diasporic audiences.

Drawing on in-depth interviews and observations at industry events focused on South Asian American media and marketing, Punathambekar's account features two protagonists. The first is Nusrat Durrani, a media executive who was largely responsible for developing the MTV-World initiative, and who understood very well that the relationship between "diaspora" and "home" was much more ambivalent for South Asian American youth compared to their parents' generation. Born and raised in North India, Durrani had worked for a decade in India and Dubai before moving to the United States and joining MTV in the early 1990s.

In Punathambekar's narrative, one that blends in-depth interviews with news and trade-press material, Durrani emerges as a figure who was part of a much broader cultural shift. Given the ethnographic tenor of the chapter, we hear Durrani reflect on his career and how his outlook was shaped by diasporic artists, associated with the Asian Underground, a music and cultural formation involving primarily second-generation British-Asian youth with ties to different countries in the Indian subcontinent. Punathambekar then pivots to explore the constraints within which someone like Durrani can act. We thus learn that despite Durrani's valiant efforts to position and brand MTV-Desi as a uniquely diasporic space, MTV Networks entered into a distribution deal with DirecTV and located MTV-Desi firmly within an India-centric programming package. This decision was partly a function of television industry professionals grappling with a changing distribution landscape in the United States, and certainly spoke to their uncertainty about a channel like MTV-Desi reaching audiences via satellite television. Thus, even though Durrani and others at MTV-Desi recognized that it would be a mistake to imagine Desi youth and their engagement with media and popular culture in the same terms as their parents, statements from others at MTV Networks revealed that this was how Desi identity continued to be mobilized.

Punathambekar also narrates other stories of diasporic media entre-preneurs growing up and coming to terms with Desi identity and culture, and proceeds to situate them in relation to policies of multiculturalism and the commodified nature of "Indo chic" or "Asian cool" in North America and the UK. The link to discourses of multiculturalism enables Punathambekar to draw attention to how media entrepreneurs' stories about their selves and their sense of being and becoming South Asian American became intimately tied to media industry logics. In the United States, these entrepreneurs' lived experiences as second-generation diasporic youth were regarded as crucial to their ability to understand the particularities of South Asian American culture, and thereby positioned them uniquely well to build commercially viable 'Desi' media businesses.

Practices of media aggregation and distribution that scholars mapped rested on logics that were largely fine-tuned in the film and television industries. By the late 2000s, these logics were being transformed under the impact of digitalization, leading in particular to the emergence of digital media companies (Spotify and Netflix, for example). In turn, this created distinct new roles for professionals, with a range of technological skills from software programming to data analytics. Developers of recommender systems that purportedly help audiences "discover" music, movies, and other content on Amazon or Netflix, for instance, have emerged as key individuals in various digital companies. Focusing on the work that developers of recommender systems do to "hook people" can shed light on a major infrastructure for contemporary media circulation. As Nick Seaver (2018) puts it in his ethnographic study of software developers and roles like that of a "chief scientist" in a streaming music company: "Small and otherwise unremarkable actions, like picking a movie to watch or changing the radio station, are the target of an exceptionally large and intricate scientific–industrial complex, which only continues to grow in size and scope" (2).

Seaver's insights into the various positions that individuals can occupy in relation to the development of algorithmic music recommender systems in the United States emerge out of fieldwork conducted over a period of five years (2011 to 2016). Moving across a range of sites including corporate offices, university labs, and academic conferences, Seaver carefully tracks how his informants' own understanding of "recommendation" shifted over time in response to rapidly evolving industry needs. As assumptions about users' underlying ratings measures came to be questioned and as new data infrastructures were put in place, software developers began making sense of their work as one of designing recommender systems that would "capture" and hold users and user interest in place. In richly theorized sections that draw on anthropological theory about animal traps to reflect on infrastructures of "capture," Seaver weaves in accounts of how informants' role as developers evolved (from "coder" to "manager," for instance) as the algorithmic systems became complicated over time.

Across these cases, we see how individual workers and professional roles serve the crucial industrial function of enabling the circulation of media. Moreover, these cases show that "circulation" necessarily entails the spatial logics of movement, as media products move from one place to another, and scale, from the local to the global. This scholarship shows that specific people in certain professional positions manifest these logics in concrete ways. Moreover, the cases examined here demonstrate how meanings and associations connected to media texts and products are not only generated at the site of production, but also in the process of their dissemination. Whether theorizing them as "intermediaries" or not, this scholarship on media circulation highlights key media professionals' ability to move media through the world and, in the process, inflect media with specific cultural values and meanings.

Stitching the Industry Together: Talent Agents and Agencies

The contemporary film and television industries can be described as "post-Fordist." Although dominated by a small number of major corporations that control distribution and broadcast, they are fed by numerous smaller, sub-contracted, and specialized firms, such as independent production houses, computer graphics and effects firms, prop rental companies, and so on. And because almost all film and television production happens on a "project" basis, much effort must be made to coordinate the talent for such projects, such as actors and actresses, writers, and directors. Filling this crucial role – and many others as well – is the talent agent.

Of all the different sectors within Hollywood, talent agencies have proven exceptionally opaque. Yet two studies have overcome this difficulty and provided thorough examinations of the crucial role talent agents play within Hollywood: Tom Kemper's *Hidden Talent* (2009) and Violaine Roussel's *Representing Talent* (2017). Yet these books differ considerably from one another in research methods, materials, and analytical approaches, and thus show the multiple ways one can make arguments about specific industrial roles and individuals. Whereas Kemper's study is historical, Roussel's is contemporary (from 2010 to 2015). Kemper's work derives from trade press and archival records from within the industry, while Roussel's work is based on interviews with industry professionals and observations of work activities. And whereas Kemper's work falls within the tradition of the "new film history," Roussel's is a work of sociology. Despite these differences, there is fascinating overlap in the insights into talent agents provided by these books.

Hidden Talent details the rise of Hollywood talent agents in the late 1920s and demonstrates the integral role they played within the studio system through the 1950s. Influenced by "economic sociology," the book makes use of trade press as well as agents' personal and business documents held in various archives. This access to internal documents allows Kemper to detail the personal and career histories of specific agents, including the two biggest agents of the time, Myron Selznick and Charles Feldman. Through these cases, Kemper is able to generalize about the industrial niche agents filled within Hollywood as well as their common work duties and practices, such as negotiating contacts and expanding personal and professional networks. Kemper shows how "personality" was intertwined within agents' professional activities, as agents "exemplify the modern practice of marketing personality, of selling one's self" (73). Filled with stories regarding specific individuals punctuated by rich details regarding particular business transactions, as well as larger observations regarding the structural composition of the talent agencies and Hollywood, *Hidden Talent* shows how different individuals forged the industrial role of the Hollywood agent.

Representing Talent provides a thorough portrait of the contemporary workings of talent agents, which differs theoretically from Kemper's book. Roussel spent five years studying agents in Los Angeles, interviewing over one hundred and even shadowing a few in their work routines; she credits her "outsider" status as a French social scientist with gaining such intimate access to an otherwise guarded social group. Her interview material appears throughout her analysis as illustration of her various larger points, and all these quotes are anonymous. As a work of sociology, the book is more interested in providing generalized descriptions of talent agents' social roles, relationships, and professional networks than in providing specific narratives or concrete examples.

Roussel identifies many of the same characteristics of "agenting" as Kemper, including the role played by personality, the necessity of maintaining "relationships" with talent that are defined by a "tension between professionality and intimacy" (103), as well as differences between "big" and smaller agencies. Roussel shows how agents are trained and professionalized at various stages of the institutional hierarchy, and goes in depth over several chapters about the "relationship work" they engage in with their clients. This work entails complex social and professional activities related to trust, money, taste, and creativity. Roussel aims to disrupt the notion that Hollywood is divided between "creative" and "business" labor by characterizing talent agents as forming "evaluation communities." She asserts that agents are "collectively engaged in the evaluation of quality and the definition of value of people and projects," which requires an understanding that the "economic and symbolic dimensions of value creation" are intertwined (27).

Thus, while this book does not provide the detail or financial data of Kemper's historical study, it illuminates the economic, social, and creative function that talent agents serve within the movie industry. Indeed, despite the differences in their research materials, methods, and timeframes, both of these studies illuminate much of the work that talent agents and agencies do. As noted, this entails significant bridging of multiple aspects of the American movie industry, connecting creative workers to the producers and distributors that make and circulate movies; in Kemper's case, he shows how talent agents developed a surprisingly important position within the classic Hollywood system, while Roussel similarly shows how agents and production professionals are "tied together in antagonistic positions" in their mutual attempt to access and control talent (36). Just as important, these studies of talent agents both illustrate how an individual professional role does not just serve an important function within an industry, but more that certain figures help to connect multiple workers in different positions to form a greater industrial network.

Conclusion

Although research about individuals and professional roles may have been less common in twentieth-century media industries scholarship, this chapter has highlighted numerous cases that reveal the benefits of organizing an industrial study, or part of a study, in this manner. Indeed, if the cases discussed in this chapter appear wide-ranging, this likely results from the fact that the media industries are made up of many, many different individuals and professional roles, all of which serve important, often highly specialized functions within larger industries. The breadth of the scholarship, in other words, mirrors the breadth of different kinds of industrial workers and roles. It seems that this type of research is truly only limited by the interest and imagination of the researcher in searching out and identifying additional, but under-discussed figures and roles that impact how media gets made, circulated, sold, and so on. Other studies might examine achievements of some specific person that have otherwise been overlooked by scholars, or whose example broadens or changes our understandings of the media industries more generally. The possibilities seem boundless, particularly as changes within the organization of different media businesses alter how workers do their jobs – or create entirely new professional positions and roles.

Likewise, the cases discussed in this chapter reveal the range of research methods and materials that one can use in the study of media professionals and their functions, from interviews and participant observation to discourse analysis of diverse archival materials. Identifying a media professional or industrial role can be just the beginning of a project. One must then determine how to study that individual or role, which presents another set of methodological questions that will inevitably shape the resulting analysis, as the cases discussed in this chapter demonstrate.

Moreover, the cases examined in this chapter all endeavor, in different ways, to show how understanding a media worker or professional role provides a new understanding of the larger industry in question – or even how their study informs our knowledge of the conditions of the media *industries*. Thus industrial study of individuals and roles within the media often have a double charge: first, to provide a clear, detailed portrait of that specific individual or role and, second, to demonstrate how these figures illustrate traits or issues facing media industries. Just as the underlying research question is often an important source of connection with existing intellectual conversations that is broader than the specific industry under study, looking for parallels among similar roles in different industries can offer new insight to media industry studies generally.

Although this chapter considers a wide variety of roles, the even more significant note to take is the breadth of questions that might be explored concerning all those roles. There are still many roles that critical scholarship lacks much account of – the books on agents by Kemper and Roussel, as well as Raymond Boyle's (2018) recent account of the *Talent Industry,* have only recently rectified what had been a significant, longstanding gap in understanding the role agents play in decisions about which films and television are made and why they take the forms they do.

Further, we opened this chapter by noting the extensive presence contemporary media moguls play in our understanding of media. But even though media moguls feature prominently in news and trade press coverage across the world, recent scholarship indicates how much more we stand to learn. In *Arab Media Moguls* (2015), for instance, Donatella Della Ratta, Naomi Sakr, and Jakob Skovgaard-Petersen point out that "media mogul" can be a productive analytical term and open up new questions for media industry studies instead of just shoring up orientalist assumptions about autocratic regimes and tightly controlled media systems. Surveying shifts in the Arab media region over the past twenty years, contributors to *Arab Media Moguls* examine how "political authoritarianism, oil economies, religious revivalism, and political turmoil" (6) shaped the emergence of media moguls. The result is a wide-ranging look at issues pertaining to the operations of contemporary media industries – "the role of family in business and the issue of succession ... the kinds of risk taken, hiring and firing strategies, access to finance and approaches to debt ... each mogul's relationship to the inner circles of political power, the opportunities provided by steps toward relaxation of media monopolies, the place of media in the mogul's business empire and the nature of the medium on which the empire was built" (2015, 6). Put simply, an inquiry into one specific individual can spiral outward to reveal a whole host of complex political-economic, social, and cultural dynamics that shape media industries across a world region.

There remain many questions to ask about roles that do have a more expansive history of analysis. Identifying particular roles or individuals as a study interest is often a first step that then requires narrowing to a particular research question about the role. That research question often identifies the scholarly conversation one aims to join with their research. While much of the conversation may be particular to existing research about the role, it is also important to consider how a similar question may have guided research in relation to different roles and even different industries.

One notable research question that scholars have asked of media workers is less about how different individuals and groups perform their labor and serve industrial functions, but is more interested in how they formulate themselves as a *cultural* field with distinctive practices of meaning-making. This "production culture" research is the subject of the following chapter.

3

"Production" Cultures

Some media industry scholarship examines media practitioners and the site of their labor as "production cultures," in order to explore communities of media work that constitute important cultural fields in their own right. Such research is wide ranging. Like other strands of media industry study, production cultures research is motivated by the notion that *how* media gets made influences *what* media is made, but focuses especially on the meanings and values that shape the people who shape the media. It examines the ways in which media workers constitute themselves as a community and analyzes these communities' beliefs, values, priorities, practices, and rituals. In some production cultures work, in fact, the making of media can appear rather tangential and it takes on the character of a labor study set in the context of a site of media making.

While the distinction of production cultures as a category of media industry study is at best loosely observed, we suggest that production cultures research can be distinguished from many other studies of media industry workers and professional roles by this more anthropological interest in workers' meaning-making activities. Whereas the previous chapter studied individuals and roles in terms of their service to or function within a media organization, production cultures is less interested in how people serve industrial functions but rather in the cultural values and logics that orient these people as industrial workers. This subtle but important difference can be illuminated through juxtaposing two hypothetical studies. In one – more characteristic of the projects discussed in the last chapter – the researcher asks: "What role does the showrunner play in contemporary television production? What does their work entail, what power do they have, and what resources do they make use of to perform these tasks? What challenges do they face? What position does the showrunner hold in relation to other professionals involved in the production and distribution of television?" In a production cultures study, the researcher might ask: "What does the showrunner *think* about their work? How do they define themselves as television workers? What motivates them to work in the way they do? What are the cultural values that guide showrunners' common daily practices, and how do they express those values to themselves and others? What kinds of stories do they tell about their work, and what are the underlying values that these stories convey? What are the key objects and rituals through which showrunners organize themselves as a distinct community within the television industry?"

This work has increasingly identified itself, or been identified as production cultures or production studies. We use the former here because it best distinguishes the feature that differentiates this scholarship – what we describe as analysis of cultures of practice among specific communities of media workers. There has been a noticeable increase in research about production cultures, particularly John Thornton Caldwell's *Production Culture* (2008) and two edited collections, *Production Studies* (Mayer, Banks, and Caldwell, 2009) and *Production Studies: The Sequel!* (Banks, Conor, and Mayer, 2015) and in single authored work by volumes' editors, Caldwell, Vicki Mayer, Miranda Banks, and Bridget Conor. In their introduction to the first *Production Studies* collection, the editors identify production studies as an interdisciplinary project that draws its "intellectual impetus from cultural studies," and maintains cultural studies' interest in analyzing "relationships of power" (2). Indeed, like many other studies of media workers, production cultures is concerned with issues of power, social identity, and culture in a broad sense. This interest in power and culture can include discussions of the gendering of labor and professional experiences, for instance, or the way in which media workers manifest anxieties related to rapid technological change or economic constraints.

What sets production cultures apart in this regard, however, is the concerted interest in revealing the everyday experiences in which power and agency actually operate for a range of different industrial workers, who are organized in relation to other industrial workers. As the editors of *Production Studies* also write, production cultures work examines "how media producers make culture and, in the process, make themselves into particular kinds of workers in modern, mediated societies," particularly by looking at how these workers "form communities of shared practices, languages, and cultural understandings of the world" (2). Here, the editors spell out that production cultures is interested in work practices as well as cultural norms among media workers. For some, theorizing work and labor conditions take priority over analyzing the significance of those labor conditions to its impact on what media are made.

From a methodological perspective, there can be considerable overlap between studying production cultures and other studies of industrial roles or individuals that we consider in other chapters and, indeed, some works verge into production cultures while organizing themselves to explicate other levels of analysis. In this respect, "production cultures" appears to be a way of interpreting media workers – and interpreting these workers' self-understandings. We recognize that these distinctions appear porous, and in many cases, work discussed in other chapters could fit here, just as the work described as characteristic of production cultures might also be placed elsewhere. Yet there is also a sense of a distinction to this work that we found valuable to attempt to tease out.

Further, although "production cultures" or "production studies" are how this approach is commonly referenced, we don't understand it as only concerned with the tasks related to making media – the "production" in "production cultures" is a signifier that includes a much broader range of media worker than solely those who *make* films, television programs, video games, and so on. We thus include a section on production cultures work that is more precisely described as circulation cultures.

This chapter opens with a range of research by anthropologists studying different film industry sectors. The methods and approaches developed by cultural anthropologists have been particularly important in the development of production cultures research. We then turn to some production cultures publications to reflect on the particular methodological guidance they offer and then survey research that considers an expansive range of audiovisual production cultures. While "production cultures" studies of circulation are less common, they exist and are helpful in adding detail to our understanding of media circulation. The chapter concludes with a brief consideration of some research that might be considered as production cultures that take aim outside of audiovisual industries in an effort to illustrate the broad application of this approach that has been mostly associated with the study of film and television.

Anthropologists and Cinema Production Worlds

Given that production cultures seeks to understand how media workers engage in cultural practices at the same time they engage in industrial activities, this area of research is more heavily influenced by anthropology than other types of media industry research. Methodologically, it is common for production cultures work to rely on interviews and participant observation. In fact, anthropologists have produced some important production cultures scholarship. Powdermaker, as discussed in Chapter 1, provides one of the earliest and most substantial production cultures studies in her book, *Hollywood, the Dream Factory: An Anthropologist Looks at the Movie-Makers* (1950). Prior to studying media professionals, Powdermaker had studied communities in what is now Papua New Guinea as well as the American South. During 1946–1947, she spent more than a year in Los Angeles, interviewing around nine hundred people working in the film industry. These interviews were semi-directed and took place in professional settings, private homes, as well as at restaurants and similar public locations. Powdermaker focused her study on "above the line" workers, including executives, producers, directors, actors, and writers, and, unlike Ortner and Caldwell (as detailed below), she found this strata of workers to be accessible and forthcoming regarding their experiences. She asserts: "All human beings love to talk about themselves and are flattered at having their opinions taken seriously;" more pointedly she states: "The level of frustration [among Hollywood workers] was high, and frustrated people love to talk" (6). However, Powdermaker wrote most of her notes about her interviews immediately after they had concluded, as she found that her subjects were less talkative when she took notes during a conversation.

Much of Powdermaker's study is organized around particular professional roles, with chapters devoted specifically to executives, producers, writers, actors, and so on, which she book-ends with chapters that articulate broader claims regarding Hollywood's social organization, its defining cultural characteristics and beliefs, and the way in which this culture impacts the kinds of films that get made. Powdermaker's ultimate goal, in fact, is to make claims regarding the social impact of movies on American culture, and she is concerned about how the culture inside Hollywood might affect the culture of the nation.

In this regard, Powdermaker is highly critical and even disparaging. Sounding very much like Max Horkheimer and Theodor Adorno, whose critique of the culture industry appeared around the time that she was working in Los Angeles, Powdermaker concludes: "Hollywood represents totalitarianism" (327). In her estimation, Hollywood embodies such totalitarian characteristics as "the concept of people as property and as objects to be manipulated, highly concentrated and personalized power for power's sake, an amorality, and an atmosphere of breaks, continuous anxiety and crises" (332).

Indeed, although *Hollywood, the Dream Factory* presents a "behind-the-scenes" picture of the social world that makes movies, one gets the clear sense that this world is riven by chronic dysfunction. As Powdermaker represents it, Hollywood is defined by the economic and symbolic power of money at the expense of artistic skill or creativity, by perpetual insecurity and anxiety on the part of some workers, and by arrogance and bad judgment on the part of others, as well as "magical thinking" that leads workers at every level to "attribute their own and other people's success to forces lying beyond their control in the world of chance" (284). In the face of such negative and sweeping assessments, contemporary media industry studies scholars can still appreciate Powdermaker's work on a number of levels: for the scale and duration of her study; for her fine-grain attention to specific professional roles and even individual workers (all of whom she keeps anonymous through the use of quippy nicknames like the screenwriter "Mr. Cynic" or the director "Mr. Well Adjusted"); and thinking holistically about how worker practices and beliefs shape textual forms and society more generally. All the same, contemporary media industry scholars have the benefit of more nuanced models of ideology, structure, agency, and self-mediation than Powdermaker's work offers.

Whereas Powdermaker found above-the-line Hollywood workers accessible and talkative, Ortner encountered significant resistance when she attempted to engage in a similar anthropological study of movie professionals more than sixty years later (Ortner, 2009, 178; Ortner, 2013, 2–3). In contrast, Ortner found that the social world of "independent" or "indie" cinema was much more accessible, thus indie cinema is the subject of her production cultures study, *Not Hollywood*. In addition to studying a different worker community than Powdermaker, Ortner's work is distinctive in its reflexive research method and for examining a range of materials that extend beyond her interviews and participant observation.

In her contribution to the *Production Studies* edited collection, Ortner claims that examining the independent cinema production cultures entails "studying sideways," because the people who work in indie film share the scholar's social position among the "knowledge classes" (2009, 183). For Ortner, this forces the researcher to reflect on "the complicity between us and our informants" as well as "our own elite status" (184). In general, one must acknowledge that there are hierarchies within academia too – not all researchers are uniformly "elite" and issues of scholars' positionality in relation to research sites and subjects need to be worked out with great reflexivity.

In the resulting book *Not Hollywood*, Ortner identifies her method as "interface ethnography," which entails looking at how a relatively guarded community, in this case media workers in the field of independent cinema, interfaces with the public (2013, 26). Thus in addition to personal interviews, Ortner's book draws from her observations from

"Q&A sessions, public interviews, and panels" (27). Ortner also spends several chapters in the book examining film texts for their content and style. In these analyses, Ortner treats these films as public manifestations of indie production cultures, adopting an approach toward anthropological research inspired by Clifford Geertz (as does John Thornton Caldwell, as detailed below). Within this "Geertzian framework," the researcher can look at an incredibly wide range of materials as "texts," including interviews, observations, and cultural events and products of a community, and analyze how they reveal a group's "distinctive ways of thinking about their work and their world" (2013, 27).

Ortner argues that the world of independent film production is "in the business of 'cultural critique,'" by providing a comparatively more sophisticated, mission-driven, creative, and critical cinema that defines itself in opposition to Hollywood (10). She highlights the values and beliefs that this community celebrates and uses to distinguish itself, including "passion" and edginess; she coordinates her assertion regarding this last point with extended textual analyses of dark and morally ambiguous films. Ortner also provides a sense of some of the work practices involved in making independent films, as she details how independent producers discursively and industrially build up a film's critical and cultural "value."

In addition to providing insights into the practices and beliefs of indie cinema production cultures and for demonstrating the relevance of diverse materials for anthropological analysis, *Not Hollywood* is also notable for how Ortner, like Powdermaker before her, aims to connect independent cinema to larger social forces and places filmmaking in a broader political economy. Specifically, Ortner asserts that the independent film world is a particular manifestation of and reaction against the effects of neoliberal social and economic policies since the 1970s. In this respect, both Powdermaker and Ortner seek to make large-scale, structural arguments more typical of critical political economy through the process they use to make more localized and anthropological research and analyses.

Anthropological studies of media production cultures can acquire additional significance when we look beyond the American context and to methodologies focused on observing the practices of filmmaking. Tejaswini Ganti's (2012) ethnographic study of the Mumbai-based Hindi film industry's production culture stands out in the domain of global studies of media and communication for constructing richly detailed and theorized accounts of everyday practices of different communities within the film industry. Ganti's work speaks to how production cultures research can connect everyday work culture in a particular setting to broad concerns about an industry at large.

In one passage, Ganti provides a sketch of a typical day on a film set. The sketch is a "composite," as she puts it, and is based on her observations of a variety of film shoots across many years of field research in Mumbai. Ganti gives readers a palpable sense of the filmmaking process, capturing the repetitious nature of film production, the seemingly interminable wait for a brief sequence of shooting, and even the boredom that sets into routine tasks. The same routines, conversations between different individuals on the set – the director and his many assistant directors, the producer and his sons who are foisted onto the beleaguered director as apprentices, a screenwriter, an aspiring actor, and so on – offer glimpses into the "structure, organization, and social relations of the film industry" (155) as a whole. As her analysis continues, Ganti builds on her observations on film sets through interviews conducted with professionals across the production and distribution sectors and trade press materials to reflect more broadly and theorize the production culture of the Hindi film industry. Through these many forms of evidence, she is able to identify, "the prevalence of face-to-face interactions, the significance of kinship as a source of talent, the set as a meeting space, the highly oral style of working, and the very visible manifestations of hierarchy" (156).

This methodology allows her to build arguments about the power roles and the operation of power within a media sector. Ganti's ethnography reveals a hybrid terrain of media production characterized by family businesses and established social networks. She identifies how these entities reformulate their identities to meet the demands of new circuits of capital as well as a range of media corporations seeking to make inroads into Bollywood only to find themselves contending with the limits of corporate logics in the Bombay film industry. Her account of the "gentrification" of the Hindi film industry in a range of sites, roles, and practices – casting, the power wielded by distributors, social relations that serve gatekeeping functions, etc. – helps us move beyond explanations of media change that are either state-centric or invoke the overpowering influence of transnational media companies.

Ganti's anthropological approach toward production cultures research thus provides rich material from which we can account for local difference, the imbrication of such difference within trans-national circuits of capital, and crucially, how political-economic, cultural, and technological change forces industries to recalibrate themselves at every level, including daily work culture. It demonstrates how individuals in different roles in the Hindi film industry make sense of and articulate highly situated responses to the structural and industry-wide changes that they had to negotiate, beginning in the 1990s, as economic reforms led to major transformations in the media and communication industries in India.

Although Powdermaker, Ortner, and Ganti conducted their research in different historical moments and in different parts of the world, their work demonstrates a consistent interest in assessing the values and beliefs that orient different film production communities. In each of these cases, we see how an anthropological approach toward culture can provide new and interesting insights into the media industry, particularly by indicating how media workers' beliefs get manifested, circulated, and interconnected with larger industrial structures, social networks, and cultural forces. Although many researchers who engage in media industries projects might not be formally trained as anthropologists, studies like Powdermaker's, Ortner's, and Ganti's demonstrate the utility in making use of anthropological research methods and analytical frames.

Cultural Studies of Audiovisual Media Production

There have been several notable cases of scholars trained in film, television, or media studies that have developed robust and sophisticated methods for researching industry workers from a cultural perspective. As we indicated in Chapter 1, Stuart Hall's encoding/decoding theoretical model opened up the possibility for studying media production as a "determinate moment" of meaning making, and yet for many years scholars working within a cultural studies paradigm looked more consistently at audiences and the complexities of media reception. Although "production" remained a consistent element of the various theoretical models that elaborated and complicated Hall's conceptualization, few cultural studies or media studies scholars looked concertedly at this area through the end of the 1990s. This situation changed dramatically in the last two decades, even more so since "media industry studies" coalesced in the late 2000s and made inroads into an area previously explored more by anthropologists and sociologists.

In 2001, media scholar Elena Levine published an essay that took up the charge from within cultural studies to examine the world of media production. Through an analysis of a specific case study, Levine developed general methods for researching and analyzing media production as a cultural practice, drawing in particular from Richard Johnson's circuit of culture theoretical model (67). Levine examined the production of the soap opera *General Hospital* through interviews with people working on the program and two weeks of participant observation of the show's production. Unlike Ortner, Levine found that getting this access to the show was easy, although in her case, Levine also identifies herself as a "fan" of *General Hospital* with deep subjective attachments to the show. This intimacy with the program enabled Levine to read the production scene within the context of her understanding of the show's content and style.

In her analysis of this single program, Levine examines five factors that shape the work world of the show – and thus its resulting form and content – and uses the factors as a structuring framework. First, she considers "production constraints," including the ownership of the company that produces the show, its budget, and its historical position within the soap opera genre. Second, Levine identifies the "production environment" as an important element that entails the practical demands of producing a show. In this specific case, *General Hospital* requires rapid and continuous work in order to bring it onto the air five days a week; Levine also identifies the importance of different job positions and notes the gendered division of labor among them. Third, Levine discusses "production routines and practices," which involve looking at how workers create coherent textual meanings and continuous narratives in the face of a hectic and non-linear work schedule. Fourth, she addresses "production of characters and stories," or the logistical and emotional labor that writers, actors, and others perform to create coherent narratives and characters. Fifth and finally, Levine looks at "the audience in production," or the ways in which production staff interacted with audiences and actually serve as audiences in their own right. Thus, Levine's study provides a clear understanding of the production of *General Hospital* in particular, but her work more generally provides categories for understanding some of the forces that shape media production worlds and the complexity of "meaning making" in television production.

John Thornton Caldwell has engaged in production cultures research for many years, and has developed sophisticated theoretical frames and methodological tools in this pursuit. Caldwell's work, in fact, can be distinguished from many other production studies as a result of its theoretical and methodological specificity; moreover, Caldwell is unusual in that he was also trained as a filmmaker and has made several productions in his own right. In the monograph *Production Culture* and in essays published before and after it, Caldwell articulates a distinctive approach toward the study of media production worlds, which he calls "Cultural Studies of Media Production" (2006) or "cultural studies of film/television production" (2009). As he states in the monograph, he "explores the cultural practices and belief systems of film/video production workers in Los Angeles" (1). More specifically, and contrasting with Powdermaker, Caldwell looks at the production culture of *below the line* media workers. Caldwell is interested not in deploying critical or cultural theory upon a production community in order to understand it, but rather – influenced by the anthropological work of Clifford Geertz – seeks to understand how a production community reflexively engages in self-conceptualization, self-theorization, and self-evaluation. Caldwell calls such activities on the part of media workers "critical industrial practices" (2006, 110; 2008, 5). Although Caldwell had articulated arguments along these lines in his earlier book, *Televisuality*, his later work represents the more dedicated realization of this endeavor.

In his effort to understand how production communities engage in meaning-making activities, Caldwell's work takes an unusually broadminded approach toward research materials. As he states:

> My approach is synthetic, and I examine data from four registers or modes of analysis: textual analysis of trade and worker artifacts; interviews with film/television workers; ethnographic field observation of production spaces and professional gatherings; and economic/industrial analysis. I have attempted whenever possible to keep these individual research modes "in check" by placing the discourses and results of any one register ... in critical tension of dialogue with the others. (2008, 4)

In this manner, Caldwell gathers an immense "archive" of information, which he analyzes for consistencies and contradictions. His interpretation of these data shows how the audiovisual production cultures in Los Angeles create, sustain, and interpret themselves in myriad practices and artifacts.

Indeed, Caldwell's monograph examines a sometimes-surprising range of "texts." Caldwell begins by analyzing the narratives that media workers tell about themselves and their work, and finds correspondences between these stories and the strata of the laborers; in this endeavor, Caldwell shows that the stories that media workers tell themselves are just as ideologically significant as the stories that get told in the films and television programs that workers make. He also examines the many ways in which media workers produce and behave within distinct spaces, from the architecture of corporate headquarters, to ritual spaces like pitch sessions and trade shows, to an individual's attire. Perhaps even more unusually, Caldwell reads production technologies and tools and representations thereof as "texts" that embody and convey cultural meanings for media workers at the same time as they affect work routines. Whether looking at work and communication procedures among television writers, or branding efforts on the part of media conglomerates, or "making of" features on DVDs, Caldwell's *Production Culture* uncovers numerous ways in which film and television workers make sense of themselves, their jobs, and their worlds. And while many media professionals will renounce "theory" as practiced by scholars,

Caldwell shows how these people engage in sophisticated and complex theorizations of their own.

The systematic way in which Caldwell articulates his research and interpretive method has made his work especially impactful in studies of audiovisual media production cultures. Vicki Mayer's work represents another major contribution to the area of production cultures, and takes an expansive approach toward the topic. In addition to co-editing and contributing chapters to the two edited collections on the topic, Mayer's monograph *Below the Line: Producers and Production Studies in the New Television Economy* (2011) opens the terrain for production studies into new and provocative areas and offers inspired critiques of media production – and of media studies itself. In it, Mayer examines the work cultures in four disparate sites of the media industries: television assembly workers in Manaus, Brazil; soft-core videographers; casting agents for reality television programs; and citizens who volunteer to help shape cable regulation in different localities. In selecting these sites and communities, Mayer intends to upend assumptions held within media studies, and within television studies more particularly, by showing how values such as "creativity" and "professionalism" operate outside the industrial areas that more commonly get examined.

The chapter about soft-core media makers, for instance, delves deeply into how workers define what it means to be "professional" media makers, an especially pressured attribute given these workers' marginal relationship to the mainstream American television industry. All the while, Mayer analyzes how issues of gender and power shape these workers' practices and values, as perhaps unsurprisingly, this particular community was defined by a hyper-masculinity. Alternatively, Mayer's chapter about television assembly workers in Brazil focuses on the values of a largely female workforce. Here, Mayer deconstructs the idea that "creativity" in the television business is reserved for only those prominent figures who make notable television programs by showing how the workers in television factories develop their own vital forms of creativity. For example, she notes how factory workers innovated their physical work on the assembly line in ways that kept them engaged with the otherwise monotonous work and, crucially, more efficient so as to earn work breaks. In analyses like these, Mayer shows how media workers define themselves and their priorities in meaningful ways, and yet also serve the profit motives of the employer.

Indeed, the analyses of worker communities in *Below the Line* consistently link their practices and beliefs to large-scale, political-economic conditions, or what Mayer identifies as "the new television economy." Throughout, Mayer upholds a Marxian labor theory of value, and accordingly situates her work as a critique of the contemporary social structures that produce the working conditions she describes. For all that Mayer details and analyzes the beliefs and values of different production cultures, her work in many ways can be understood as "critical political economy" through its concern for the concrete experiences of human beings engaged in industrial activity. Further, although her analysis of such workers as those manufacturing televisions might appear unusually expansive within media studies, Mayer connects these accounts with larger theoretical concerns commonly found in television and media studies.

In this respect, Mayer joins with Levine, Caldwell, and others in providing a model for conducting production cultures research within a media studies perspective. These scholars have significantly opened up the terrain for cultural studies of media production – both in terms of sites and objects of analysis as well as in interpretive method. These works provide a very clear sense that the realm of media production constitutes a rich and complex cultural field, and that methods and theories from cultural studies and media studies can help us to understand this richness and complexity.

"Circulation" Cultures

As we noted at the outset of this chapter, we don't consider the identification of this approach as production cultures as an intentional move to focus only on the making of media and not its circulation. Nonetheless, far more research has examined the cultures that surround media making than its circulation. There also seems a rather fine distinction between research that studies circulation practices through examining individuals, organizations, and industries and that which attends to something that might be conceived of as "circulation cultures." Many of the studies cited in other chapters – such as those Herbert and Brannon Donoghue explored in Chapter 2 – do explore, respectively, the cultures of the work of video store clerks and their beliefs and values, or how regional country managers and other distribution workers describe themselves and their work, but arguably do not do so to an extent that places their work firmly within this "cultures" distinction.

The day-to-day tasks of media circulation workers are far more physically diffuse than production work, so that identifying a location at which to observe the culture can be difficult. As Timothy Havens's (2006) research on television distribution fairs identifies, a lot of circulation work can be about relationship maintenance among different sectors of distributors and retailers or exhibitors. This work happens though travel and in one-on-one meetings and messaging, and may be more difficult for the observational methods of production cultures to uncover. Nevertheless, some have constructed studies clearly identifiable as characteristic of circulation cultures. In *Signal and Noise: Media Infrastructure, and Urban Culture in Nigeria* (2008), anthropologist Brian Larkin examines the cultural logics of media technologies in Northern Nigeria and how they create particular features of urban life. Larkin's examination is wide-ranging, but his exploration of the cultures that develop around the making and trade of pirate video provides an illustration of what a study of circulation culture might look like.

Perhaps it is not surprising to have studies of circulation set in a more informal market than is characteristic of many Western and highly corporatized media contexts given the difficulty of accessing corporate circulation practices. Still, Larkin begins by noting that the largely informal market that preceded Nigerian video distribution before his study had largely become formalized. Circulation cultures outside the mainstream might also provide more entry points for scholars – whether organizations such as independent book stores, news agents, or independent music distributors, as in the case of Rough Trade, explored by David Hesmondhalgh (1997) and discussed in the next chapter. Larkin's study is primarily located and tied to Kano and its Kofar Wambia market that served as a central node of informal distribution networks for Indian and Hollywood films. He studies how the market transitioned to authorized trade of domestic Hausa films at the time of his study. Larkin notes that Kano became the "regional distribution center for electronic media in Northern Nigeria and the wider Hausaphone area" – a terrain that stretched into Chad, Cameroon, Benin, Ghana, and parts of Sudan as a result of practices established in informal trade (223). Dealers based in the market sold tapes to distributors who would then supply smaller urban and rural dealers.

Larkin's focus is more on how these circulation infrastructures affect the media culture of the region – for example, how the informal tape trade allows Nigerian audiences to watch films at the same time they are released in New York or Mumbai rather than the outdated films shown on cinema screens. Nonetheless, it is clear from his deliberate account of how these systems of trade were established by informal economies and how routes to market for Indian films had shifted to traveling through official channels that make high-quality dubs are rooted in close study of the community of the distributors that had been part of these networks of circulation. In other words, Larkin's research practice likely mirrors what would be done by a media industry researcher, although his questions are not particularly representative of such study.

The focus of Larkin's account explores how the Nigerian-produced Hausa films have drawn from the informal distribution network and the financial relationships between producers and distributors that is marked by tension over risk and desire for control by both parties. Larkin also draws connection between the conditions of the circulation culture and the textual features of Hausa films, arguing: "The roots of all Nigerian film (whether in English, Hausa, or Yoruba) in piracy means that the physical quality and look of Nigerian video film has been determined by the formal properties of pirate infrastructure" (231).

Larkin's work also raises the issue of technological breakdown and need for repair, which in some ways provides a parallel to Mayer's examination of the cultures surrounding television manufacturing in Manaus, and provides a basis for emerging scholarship such as Padma Chirumamilla's (2019) ethnographic study of South Indian television repairmen and Lisa Parks's (2018) research on mobile phone repair in rural Africa. Research exploring media circulation cultures may not be as robust, but remains important and notably provides much opportunity for development. And it is clear that scholarship on the infrastructural dimensions of media technologies and cultures will be key to developing accounts of media production and circulation in relation to, as Lisa Parks puts it, "environmental, socio-economic, and geopolitical conditions" (2015, 357).

Varied Approaches to Defining a Production Culture

To this point, this chapter has focused on scholarship that attends to the cultures of *audiovisual* media production. But important production studies research has also explored other industries, and it is important to note such cases because they provide rich models for doing production studies irrespective of media industry. Looking at the music industry, for example, Keith Negus's 1992 book *Producing Pop: Culture and Conflict in the Popular Music Industry* draws from interviews with recording industry workers in Britain and the United States carried out over a four-year period. Negus investigates the phase of initial artist discovery and the standard industrial practices for nurturing that talent. His project could arguably fit at many of the levels that organize the book: the curiosity about industry norms and practices speaks to the industry level; his analysis is informed by interviews with workers in many organizations who play many different roles; and his book opens with macrolevel scene setting of the multinational organization and global reach of the popular music industry. In its totality, though, his account of artist development that includes artist acquisition, development, production, promotion, publicity, and performance can be seen as a look into the multistage production cultures of popular music. Where other examples in this chapter identify a production community of a particular strata – such as Powdermaker's above the line informants – Negus's community of study is "vertically" connected by the journey an artist travels from discovery to album release.

Notably, Negus's book concerns itself little with artists, instead focusing on the many categories of workers that shape the nature of popular music through their roles and interactions with artists. Negus frames his study using Bourdieu's concept of cultural intermediaries and focuses on the work done throughout the process, as well as with the interactions of different stages of production and circulation of popular music. Methodologically, interviews allow Negus not only to describe and explain the significance of different stages of the process but also to present the cultural world of each role in the process. Negus uses the deep understanding of process as evidence in a critique of how particular working practices have resulted in an industry that makes popular music with particular features.

Nancy Baym's (2018) *Playing to the Crowd: Musicians, Audiences, and the Intimate Work of Connection* differs significantly from Negus's, but also illustrates a production culture approach to the music industry. Baym explores the relational work that has become part of the work-life of musicians through extensive interviews with musicians – many of whom had successful careers before digital distribution and social media. The analysis weaves a long historical context – looking back to the pre-industrial origins of music – with a precise understanding of the business of recording and performing music to understand the pressures and experience musicians face in managing the emotional labor of fan expectations. Baym's book details the culture of being a musician and how that culture differs in an environment in which musicians can – and often must – engage directly with fans. Many examples of media industry studies deal with this topic, but from the vantage of industrial consequences for record labels, digital distribution services, or how recorded and performed music function as industries. In taking up a production cultures approach, Baym's account reveals how new industrial dynamics are experienced by artists and what it is like to balance music making with the emotional labor of engaging fans.

Mark Deuze's 2007 book *Media Work* addresses many similar themes as those in Negus and Baym, but does so through a starkly different organization, by focusing on media industry labor trans-industrially. Deuze's animating problematic is the changing nature of media work in digital contexts. Where Negus's book might fit at many of the levels we use to organize our account, Deuze's is difficult to place in any of them. Following introductory chapters framing central issues in the work lives of those who work in media industries and how digital technologies are affecting that work, Deuze organizes the core of his book through chapters about work in various media industries. Deuze's account uses work to connect industries as disparate as journalism, video production, advertising, and game production to make the culture(s) of media work a unifying thematic.

Deuze explores the consequences of the casualization of paid media work at the same time that digital technologies were incorporated into many aspects of everyday life and made the boundaries of work and leisure increasingly porous, particularly for those who work in media. Deuze's wide-ranging interviews seek to answer questions about what it is like to work in media in this context and how the "organization of work shapes the professional identity of those employed in the creative industries" (xi). Deuze draws insight about media work in four different industries in five different countries. Thus Deuze's lens is quite wide in comparison to many production cultures projects that draw deep insight from a particular site, but his question is quite specific and makes this scope manageable.

Conclusion

These last several examples demonstrate some of the range of production cultures research beyond audiovisual media industries, and Deuze in particular shows how production studies can examine workers and industrial communities across industries. Indeed, we hope that this chapter helps to show that, as one kind of media industry study, production cultures research can be conducted among many different kinds of workers in any number of industries. One of Caldwell's (2008) interventions, in fact, was to argue that there was significant overlap and interaction between film and television industries among the below-the-line workers he studied (9). In this regard, it is worth stressing that production studies can present challenges to the "levels" that serve as organization tools for this book.

In its focus on media production as a cultural field, expansive production cultures work can cut across industries and sectors horizontally, can examine workers from different places in the vertical hierarchy of an individual industry, or even study media workers and working conditions broadly in relation to a significant technological change or economic issue. Alternatively, production studies can focus narrowly on a single worker community or even a single production and yet still extrapolate general tendencies of media production, such as with Levine. In its common focus on media workers and communities, production cultures may appear similar to other studies of industrial workers, roles, and groups, yet can be quite expansive in its scope, as well.

One common feature of this scholarship is the consistent interest in looking at media production as a site of meaning making – not necessarily the meanings that are made in media texts and commodities, but more in the meanings and values that media workers hold about themselves and their jobs. As this chapter shows, the interest in meaning-making activities on the part of media industry workers distinguishes production cultures from many other kinds of media industry study. This focus also leads production studies projects to engage in a wide range of research methods and to examine a variety of sources of information. Interviews with media practitioners are common, as is observation of different sites of industrial activity, including public or semi-public occasions such as trade shows and promotional events. While many kinds of media industry study might conduct similar research, production cultures work consistently aims to *interpret* such data somewhat differently, as specific manifestations of a community's cultural meanings and values. This chapter also indicates how some production studies use this analytical frame to interpret a sometimes surprisingly expansive range of materials, including technical manuals, DVD bonus features, and perhaps most unusually – cultural productions themselves, like films.

Building upon this research and analysis, the area of production cultures research continues to grow and develop in important ways. For instance, scholars have examined the production cultures in case studies from European media industries (Szczepanik and Vondereau, 2013). Others have sought to connect production studies and queer media studies (Martin, 2018), maintaining and extending the critique of power relations that is common within production culture work. As Alfred Martin indicates in the introduction to a special journal issue on the topic, queer production studies is an "offshoot" of existing work in production cultures, and examines "what it means to produce queerness in/across twenty-first-century media" (4). Specific cases of this work include David Coon's examination of the difficulties faced by a small production company that aimed to make queer media (2018), and Bryan Wuest's analysis of how distributors used promotional paratexts to shape the "queerness" of certain films (2018).

This queer production culture scholarship aligns with other recent work by Julia Himberg (2017) and Aymar Jean Christian (2018) in placing issues of gender, sexuality, and queerness more centrally within media industry research. At the same time, they continue the production cultures' project of investigating media practitioners' industrial work as cultural activities, expanding an area of media industries research that illuminates the cultural lives, practices, meanings, and values of those people who make and circulate the media that shape the meanings and values of culture at large.

4

Organizations

Moving more deeply through the levels of media industry structures next brings us to the different types of organizations that make up media industries. In recorded music, "labels" dominate production and, until recently, have also played a key role in distribution that has increasingly been taken over by organizations utilizing internet distribution such as Spotify and Apple Music. Likewise, the production process of both film and television has been dominated by organizations such as studios or production companies that have also played a significant role in distribution. Movie theaters are also organizations involved in the broader film industry, although production studios garner far more scholarly attention. Of course, these are just some of the most readily identifiable organizations. Media industries utilize countless others that engage in tasks as wide ranging as marketing, audience measurement, and labor representation, which are also meaningful organizational sites to consider.

Organizational-level studies examine specific companies or institutions that typically operate in one or more domains of a media industry and that change over time in response to economic, technological, and cultural forces. Studying organizations reveals more particular information about the practices of media companies – how they function and perform core tasks – that is only generally glossed in industry-level studies and might be unclear when studies focus on particular roles within organizations. Research at this level might seek to explain the interconnection among roles within an organization or how they negotiate various pressures from those that employ them, how they assert agency in their tasks, and the simple, yet powerful constraints that shape how and what they do. Of course, in the context of media industry studies, these questions are animated by curiosity about how these inter-organizational functions and negotiations contribute to ideas about artistic autonomy, the impact of industrial processes on creativity, and other issues related to the production and circulation of cultural goods.

Research at this level often provides "thick description" and detailed accounts of a particular organization. Its aim is depth and, although the findings on the whole may not be generalizable to other organizations, in most cases such studies do still provide broader insights on the dynamics within similar organizations. For example, Georgina Born's 2004 study of the British Broadcasting Corporation drew from 220 interviews and many hours observing people at work at the BBC over eight years. Findings of the organizational dynamics of the BBC will not perfectly predict the operation of, say, the Danish public broadcaster (DR), but it will explain general practices and issues that structure the operations of a public broadcaster, and these practices are likely relevant to understanding radio and television broadcasting, even outside of the context of public service.

Still other types of organizational studies may aim to produce knowledge generalizable across the sector, such as the cultural negotiations at stake in how studios, labels, or newsrooms operate. The research methods likely vary given that such claims require investigating multiple organizations in order to gain a more expansive base of knowledge.

The study of media organizations has been heavily influenced by media sociology and organizational studies, and there are links here to other fields including psychology and communication studies. In the United States, Paul Hirsh (1972) wrote one of the first accounts of "creative industries" that aimed to understand the dynamics of the supply chain of media industries, or how different organizations relate to each other and interact through gatekeepers and distributors. Another sociologist, Richard A. Peterson, who describes his approach as the "production of culture perspective," investigates the constraints of factors such as law, technology, market, organizational structure, and occupational careers in examining media industries (Peterson, 1982; Peterson and Anand, 2004). Various studies of news organizations in Britain in the late 1970s and early 1980s began to bring a more media-specific lens to organizations and to consider aspects of cultural power in their products. And Joseph Turow (1992), whose early text on *Media Systems in Society* brought organizational studies firmly within communication studies in the United States, describes his research as driven by investigating how power moves within, between, and among the organizations responsible for creating and circulating media and how these relations affect what is produced and how it is made available to audiences. In early research,

Turow (1982) sought to explore the organizational and interorganizational conditions that might be tied to the uncommon production of "unconventional" programs, thus linking organizational behavior to media texts.

This chapter focuses on scholarship about film studios, newsrooms, and record labels. We limit the range of organizations presented in order to hint at the breadth of questions that can be asked while attempting to hold organizational context constant. A key point here is also the diverse array of methods employed and types of questions posed, and we try to emphasize the strategic pivots scholars make in response to the availability of different sources of information. As the variation here illustrates, there is no single way to approach the industrial study of media organizations. While published accounts necessarily achieve some level of success, it is important to reflect on how the deliberate crafting of the research projects to align the methodology with the research question accounts for the achievements of these works. Readers rarely know how and where research projects start, and it is often the case that initial interests must be massaged or approached from different angles in response to limitations encountered in accessing needed sources and information.

Studios in Context

Histories of specific movie studios constitute a relatively common form of film historiography, and such books often take a specific film company as the protagonist in a story about industrial developments, challenges, and changes over a specific period of time. For the researcher, these studies are appealing because they offer a clearly delineated object of study: one company, one timeframe. For the reader, the benefits of such scholarship are many. For one, these studies can get into details of specific business practices and events that industry-scaled books often do not. Further, getting a detailed history of one movie company can be very illuminating about the movie industry in general. Indeed, sometimes this type of industrial study uses a specific company to make larger claims about "the industry," such as with Alisa Perren's *Indie, Inc.: Miramax and the Transformation of Hollywood* (2012) detailed below. Perren's and similar studio-oriented books often discuss the actions and practices of other relevant companies operating at the same strata. Likewise, some studio-based scholarship examines larger, industry-scaled or cultural events and changes in order to better understand the context in which the specific studio operated. Yet, even as these works lay out broader industrial or cultural contexts, or consider other companies, they remain focused on a single company.

It is helpful to compare two specific examples of studio-based industrial histories to see how such works can make use of different research materials, examine different timeframes, and articulate different sorts of arguments. One example is Tino Balio's work on United Artists. In 1976, Balio published *United Artists: The Company Built by the Stars*, which examines the company's history from its founding in 1919 to 1951. Eleven years later, he published *United Artists: The Company that Changed the Film Industry*, which examines the company from 1951 through its acquisition by MGM in 1981. Although there are industrial and historiographical reasons for dividing this history into two books, this separation also speaks to a fundamental aspect of the research from which they derive.

Balio's work on United Artists resulted from his access to copious primary sources, including internal United Artists documents and correspondence. As he notes in the Preface to the first book, he acquired an immense amount of corporate records from the studio in 1969 – when they became the property of the Wisconsin Center for Film and Theater Research – and this material went up to 1951. Balio's second book was based on an addition to the collection made later by the studio, and this new material ran through 1980. Thus each book derives from Balio's access to different archival materials.

One of the most striking aspects of Balio's work is its grounding in internal studio documentation. This is rare, because as he notes, film studios consistently treat "their business affairs as closely guarded secrets" (xiv). As scholars of contemporary Hollywood know, it is pretty much impossible to get detailed internal information from a studio today. (Publicly leaked documents, such as with the material released from the Sony hack of 2014 [and used in Fritz, 2018], is an exception, although using such material for research raises a number of ethical and methodological questions.) Accordingly, many of the most detailed industrial studies of film and film companies are historical rather than contemporary because there are material archives available. Such archives are few and can hold very limited materials that are sometimes difficult to access or search. Yet, in Balio's case, he had extraordinary access to internal studio documents, and he supplemented his archive research with interviews with some of the key figures at United Artists including then-chairman Arthur Krim and Charlie Chaplin. Like many who write industrial histories, Balio also made use of film industry trade publications. But his United Artists books are marked by the author's intimate access to what is so commonly held "behind the scenes."

Although rich in details, the first book, *The Company Built by the Stars*, does not articulate a strong argument about United Artists' significance within the larger film industry or movie culture. Rather, the book allows readers to understand implicitly the company's distinctiveness and significance. United Artists was an unusual company within Hollywood. Unlike other studios that controlled film production, distribution, and exhibition, United Artists was a partnership formed by a handful of the industry's top talent – actors Mary Pickford, Charlie Chaplin, and Douglas Fairbanks, as well as director D. W. Griffith – to enable the production and distribution of their movies, and in response to studio norms of the time. Over the decades, the company accrued new partners and experienced different regimes of executive leadership, and also distributed films by other individuals and companies. United Artists was also differentiated by its lack of production facilities or studio lot, and the company had to coordinate with the major studios to get its films booked in major theaters.

Balio's first volume is largely driven by specific people and business deals. Notably, the book also includes precise financial information such as dollar amounts for business transactions as well as details regarding deal negotiations. Balio frequently situates this narrative of United Artists' practices and historical development within the context of the larger movie industry, at times detailing the actions of competing companies, the financial situation of the industry, major technological changes, such as the coming of synchronous sound, or legal and self-imposed regulations that shaped industry business practice.

The second volume, *The Company that Changed the Film Industry*, also details the hopes and decisions of specific individuals, business deals and arrangements, and the changing composition of the company, and places these developments at United Artists in the context of larger happenings within the movie industry. In keeping with its subtitle, this book makes a clearer claim regarding United Artists' place and importance to the postwar film business. Balio argues that UA was a "pacesetter of the industry and started a revolution in the motion picture business" over the course of the 1950s to 1970s (3). The studio's focus on releasing independently produced films facilitated the larger shift toward independent production and studio distribution of films that would characterize Hollywood practice during this time.

Balio's books about United Artists demonstrate the nuts and bolts workings of a specific Hollywood organization, in detail made possible by having access to internal corporate documents. Perren's *Indie Inc.* shows that one can also write a compelling analysis of a single company without access to such material. Perren's book examines the prominent place that Miramax held within the American film industry during the 1990s, releasing a number of low-budget or "indie" films that gained exceptional press and acclaim, including *sex, lies, and videotape* (1989), *The Piano* (1993), and *Pulp Fiction* (1994). One of a film distributor's most important functions is marketing and promoting films, and Perren's work demonstrates that Miramax was savvy at marketing specialty films. Despite their "niche" status, many Miramax releases earned significant revenue, although never on par with major Hollywood releases. Miramax consequently "played a major role in transforming Hollywood during the 1990s" (3), specifically by signaling to the larger Hollywood studios that specialty films could be lucrative. Miramax's success led Disney to acquire it in 1993 and "every other major media conglomerate" subsequently responded by "launching their own specialty division or acquiring an existing independent distribution company" (4). As a result, many of the "indie" films released during the decade were officially part of the Hollywood system.

Like many contemporary studies of film companies and the movie business, Perren's book relies upon publicly available film industry trade publications and related websites such as *Variety*, *Hollywood Reporter*, and *indiewire.com*. Perren's book differentiates itself explicitly from Peter Biskind's journalistic and sensationalized portrait of the indie movie business, *Down and Dirty Pictures* (2004), which draws from interviews in its critique of Miramax's impact on movie culture. While *Indie Inc.* does not have "behind-the-scenes" information regarding specific individuals or business deals, Perren is nevertheless able to account for Miramax's historical development and make assertions regarding the company's business strategies and practices in a measured and precise way. It is also worth noting that Perren conducted the research for *Indie Inc.* long before Miramax co-founder Harvey Weinstein was arrested in 2018 following numerous reports of sexual abuse.

The book is almost entirely focused on the 1990s, so that most of the chapters examine a relatively short timeframe of one or two years. This allows Perren to engage in detailed analyses of the marketing and performance of specific, representative Miramax films from these moments, and to make claims about the company's strategies and shifting priorities at these junctures. Perren also examines the activities of competing companies, such as New Line Cinema and October Films, at various points in the book. This enables her to outline the broader "indie" film sector at the time and distinguish Miramax's unique position within it. Perren's focus on industrial phenomena, in fact, distinguishes *Indie Inc.* from a range of other works about independent cinema, which often focus more attention on issues of aesthetics, narrative content, and style than on industry (King 2005; Newman 2011). In this regard, one of *Indie Inc.*'s highlights is the typology it provides of the "three-tier" structure of the American film industry in the late 1990s, which consisted of the Hollywood major studios, studio-based indies, and truly independent companies (154). Although the book is primarily about the rise and fall of a single film company, her research and analysis help clarify larger phenomena defining the film industry. Like Balio's work on United Artists, it provides a clear example of how one can study a single company within the media industry from a variety of research materials and historical periods. And we arguably need more such nuanced accounts of major media companies outside the American context if we are to broaden our understanding of media history.

Media industry studies has yet to engage fully with varied trajectories and histories of film – particularly outside the "national cinemas" paradigm – in different parts of the world. In the Indian context, for instance, film and media studies has been dominated by a focus on the period after 1991 as forces of economic liberalization and cultural globalization transformed media cultures. But we have few systematic studies of film and media in the "pre-globalization" period and, where India is concerned, there are few book-length historical studies of film companies. Swarnavel Pillai's *Madras Studios: Narrative, Genre, and Ideology in Tamil Cinema* (2015) is a major achievement in this regard.

Building on primary archival research in multiple libraries and studios in India, Pillai develops what is arguably the first systematic account of film studios over a two-decade span (1937 to 1957). His focus on the studio system is particularly valuable, given that we know little about industry logics and production cultures outside the Mumbai-based Hindi language film industry (Bollywood). It is also a major contribution to the history of media capitals, given that Madras (now Chennai) was the hub of filmmaking activities for the entire southern Indian region from the 1940s through the 1960s, and remains a major center for film, television, and digital media production today. Making comparisons with studio systems in Italy, Britain, and the Soviet Union, Pillai points out that "the privately owned major Madras studios were, arguably, the largest outside the classical Hollywood system in terms of their output of films over four decades" (4). But, more importantly, Pillai does not restrict himself to a straightforward account of industry ups-and-downs; he traces links between studio system logics, star cultures, Tamil literary traditions that became crucial reservoirs of narratives and narrative techniques, and finally, changing socio-cultural and political ideologies that came to influence both film form and content. Three key chapters in the book map the industrial history of the major Madras studios before going on to analyze the aesthetics of their films.

Further, Pillai's book speaks to a larger issue confronting scholars conducting historical research in postcolonial contexts. In addition to the challenge of not having easy access to primary materials or well-organized studio archives, Pillai also had to contend with the unavailability of the films themselves. His research process thus involved spending time at multiple private and public libraries to first gather Tamil newspapers, film journals, and magazines to construct an archive pertaining to the five major studios in question. Pillai then cast a wider net to gather material from central and state government websites that provided information about studio operations and trade unions like the Southern India Cinematographers Association. Even more striking, Pillai argues that the textual readings of canonical Tamil films enabled his project of "recovering the origins of studios and their history" (5).

These three examples, that take film studios as a site of study, reveal the different foci and methods that can be employed. Despite their differences, all also use strategies to place the studios in larger historical, national, and industrial contexts, and work to expand scholarly knowledge about these particular studios at a particular time, but also inform broader understandings of the work studios do and the various competitive issues that shape the strategies they use.

News Organizations

Newsrooms have been fertile sites for organizational-level media industry study. Notably, these studies rarely focus extensively on organizational behavior, nor do they aim to expand the scholarly conversation about how organizations work. Rather, their focus is more typically on how news organizations operate in order to better understand the industrial practices that shape the daily production of news and, more broadly, shape the very idea of what constitutes "news."

Philip Schlesinger's (1978) *Putting "Reality" Together: BBC News* serves as an early example of media industries' research with a focus on news, though it was not conceived as such. Offering an example of yet another method for organizational research, Schlesinger's project is based on observations (in 1972 to 1973) of news practices and interviews with more than 120 BBC news staff. This depth of evidence allows Schlesinger to craft a multifaceted research project, and the questions he frames reveal the incredible breadth of inquiry possible at an organizational level. He lists nearly a full page of research questions in his introduction, and they illustrate the expanse of his study (12). "How did BBC News develop, and how was its growth affected by the state and by competition in the media industries? And how have these continued to affect it?" For an institution such as the BBC, this first question likely required no interviews or observation but could be completed through desk research and secondary sources. Establishing the answer to these questions nonetheless sets the stage for the more particular, original, and far-reaching analysis Schlesinger develops.

He next asks "What sort of work processes have to be gone through before a news bulletin hits the air? And is such news really the product of accidents of space and time or it is rather the result of heavily routinized activity?" These questions investigate news process to develop an understanding of the everyday production routines that shape BBC News in London. But Schlesinger is interested in more than just an account of production routines. His goal is also to reflect on how the BBC's editorial philosophy and power structures shape "newsmen" and, in turn, what is considered newsworthy. In other words, Schlesinger goes beyond rich descriptions of the production of news to develop the argument that news producers constitute an "epistemic community." News producers' particular skills, position within an organization, and occupational knowledge allow them to claim expertise that, in turn, confers "authority" and legitimacy on BBC's "news."

Schlesinger's study raised another key question: "Can 'the news' easily be changed (assuming that change is desired) or are the present structures of news broadcasting so constricting that there is little room for maneuver?" This question illustrates nicely how industry study can inform questions about texts and be connected then to issues of cultural power and authority. After investigating how the news is made and the organizational practices that lead it to take particular forms or tend toward certain characteristics, Schlesinger employs his expertise to consider how the industrial practices would need to differ in order to encourage a different result.

As the book's subtitle "BBC News" makes clear, Schlesinger is not claiming that all newsrooms or even all public service broadcast newsrooms conform to the practices and routines he observed. Nonetheless, his book is a valuable foundation for the study of other types of newsrooms, and a sophisticated reader can imagine how and why different features of his findings are likely to persist or deviate in other contexts. By grounding his study in a single context, Schlesinger may be less able to reflect on the range of features that constrain and guide an assessment of newsrooms more broadly, but his questions take full advantage of the depth of insight his methodology affords.

Pablo Boczkowski's book *Digitizing the News: Innovation in Online Newspapers* (2004) provides a different approach to organizational newsroom research. The focus of Boczkowski's book explores how print journalism gradually incorporated digital distribution and strategies. Boczkowski could have embedded himself in a particular place – as did Schlesinger – to develop deep understanding of this process of change at one institution. Instead, he uses the first few chapters to explain how US newspapers incorporated electronic publishing in the 1980s and 1990s. These chapters are partly an original history constructed through trade press and textual analysis of various early online efforts. Boczkowski identifies shifting strategies such as repurposing, recombining, and recreating, as newspapers struggled to identify the best practices of electronic news dissemination.

After these broad framing chapters, Boczkowski presents chapter-long case studies of three different newsrooms: *New York Times*, *Houston Chronicle*, and *New Jersey Online*. In contrast to Schlesinger's underlying curiosity about how the industrial features of newsgathering and preparation encourage the perpetuation of characteristics of news product, Boczkowski argues that there is not a common story to be told and that the impact of digitalization varied across different domains of news organizations.

At the *New York Times*, Boczkowski focuses on the technology section, which was the site of the paper's first experimentation with online news. He investigates the Virtual Voyager project, designed to prioritize multimedia journalism, at the HoustonChronicle.com. The Community Connection initiative of New Jersey Online reveals another strategy, one aimed at creating a platform through which readers – or users – could become content producers. Though Boczkowski does not describe the specifics of his methodology, it is apparent from his account that each case study is supported through a period of observational fieldwork and interviews. In presenting three distinct case studies, Boczkowski does not claim to address the full expanse of how print newspapers adopted digital tools. Rather, he develops careful accounts of newspapers' attempts to leverage the affordances of digital technologies and in doing so, goes on to identify the industrial factors that shaped those strategies.

Boczkowski ultimately completed his research early in what we now know to be a long and fraught process faced by US print newspapers in response to shifting distribution technologies and business models. Nonetheless, his study makes a number of valuable contributions. As an account grounded in a particular moment and particular place, his book provides an important history of the earliest efforts of print journalism to embrace the distinctive capabilities electronic journalism introduced. Secondly, his identification of three different approaches – then developed through his case studies – is able to represent a larger array of papers that also pursued one of these three strategies. Notably, he roots his demarcation of these different strategies in features of digital affordances that may have parallels in other industries and be valuable for scholars taking up the conversation of digital disruption and innovation in other media industries. Finally, Boczkowski's enumeration of the factors that shaped those approaches is also broadly valuable and may aid scholars in understanding other contexts. Subsequent scholarship in other contexts might also identify additional factors to expand the body of knowledge useful in developing theories and insights about the next technological innovation to disrupt media industries.

Sue Robinson's (2011) study of newsroom adaptation to digital change pairs well with Boczkowski's to illustrate yet other lines of inquiry. Robinson studied a single newsroom, spending 225 hours over the course of a year to observe and conduct interviews. The slight difference in Robinson's focus shifts the most strategic methodology. Robinson questions how the space of the newsroom functions differently for digital publications: "How are digital adaptations modifying news production, workflow patterns, workplace organization, and power hierarchies?" (1123–1124). In some regards, Robinson's study might be regarded as a production cultures study. Robinson selected her site because the newsroom was ceasing its print publication, as were many newsrooms at the time, and because she could be present for the full transition from print to digital.

Robinson's study captures different insights from Boczkowski's, even though their core questions are not radically different. Robinson's work identifies the daily challenges experienced by journalists as routines and duties changed. The timelines and processes for a digital publication that also seeks robust social media engagement are very different from those of a print publication. In addition to a much wider range of duties becoming part of a journalist's role, Robinson identifies shifting hierarchies and management norms within the newsroom as a certain amount of technical knowledge becomes more central. Although Robinson's journal-length account does not have the space to then explore how these changes in organizational practices and norms lead to adjustments in the news product, it is easy to imagine such a subsequent publication that ties organizational change to textual consequences.

Finally, Caitlin Petre's 2015 examination of how digital metrics reshaped journalistic work practices illustrates how organizational level study can be used to inform broader understandings of industrial practices. Petre sought to explore how metrics such as clicks, time spent on pages, and so on – new data enabled by internet distribution of news articles – shaped how journalists and editors approached their work. Her study involved observation and interviews at Chartbeat – an analytics company that supplies such metrics – as well as *Gawker* and the *New York Times*, as two rather different contexts for integrating digital metrics into the newsroom. The time spent with Chartbeat informed her research question of how metrics are produced – not so much the computational features, but how and why different measures are selected. The newsroom observation and interviews then informed her research questions of how metrics are interpreted and used in newsrooms.

Although Petre's site of analysis was particular organizations, her inquiry wasn't really about Chartbeat, *Gawker*, or the *New York Times*. Rather, these organizations were sites at which she could gain a coherent picture of how the work of journalists (individuals) and the work they produce (articles) were being affected by a shift in industrial practice (the ability to reliably gather granular data about consumption).

All of these studies focus on particular news organizations and rely on observation and interviews with those observed. Despite this commonality, the nature of their findings is wide ranging. Some tie the workings of the newsrooms to the nature of the news produced, while others investigate the implications on the lives of journalists and the way organizational changes realign the daily tasks and incentives that journalists negotiate. Digital change figures centrally in the strikingly different projects authored by Boczkowski, Robinson, and Petre, and it would be valuable to compare their insights into how digital change has affected journalists and journalism with the workers and media produced in other industries.

The Role of Record Labels in Cultural Production

Record labels have not been as common a site of organizational study as film studios or newsrooms, or at least studied in the same way. Much of the research taking this focus has examined independent and smaller labels, no doubt as a result of difficulty in gaining access to the "majors" and related to the issues that led Balio, Perren, and Pillai to their methods for investigating studios. Arguably, some of the best accounts of label practices have come from studies set at other levels. For example, Negus's (1992) account of the many stages of producing popular music does not bind itself to the operation of a particular studio, but organizes itself through the chronology of making an album, beginning with the process of talent acquisition, and following through the many roles until a completed album is marketed. Many of these are label functions, but his account isn't designed to investigate, for example, how *Sony* makes albums. Though not focused on any label in the manner of Balio's account of United Artists, the account still tells us much about the behavior and practices of labels.

Negus's 1999 book on *Music Genres and Corporate Cultures* is also relevant to an exploration of labels, without taking these organizations as his focus. Again, Negus informs his analysis through interviews with a range of music industry executives and observation of them in board-rooms and various music scenes, but the key point of differentiation Negus seeks to illuminate is not how different labels behave, as much as how the experience of artists within labels varies significantly based on music genre. Negus aims to identify the strategies of record labels, or their core logic – the identifiable patterns to practices that produce constraining forces on what music is produced and made popular – but it may be that the organization of the record label is not the most compelling site at which to explore this – at least in the case of the majors.

In one chapter, Negus compares corporate cultures at Sony, PolyGram, BMG, Warner, and others – as this was before great consolidation – and provides major label-specific analysis more comparable to other media industry organization studies. Negus sought to explore the role of culture and corporate identity for the labels and how they contribute to music production through interviews and secondary sources. Notably, this line of inquiry is relevant to the study of any media industry. Popular press journalists have constructed somewhat similar, though analytically weak accounts, of the indie film industry that likewise illustrate the importance of the mythology of different studios (Biskind, 2004). Moreover, the different perceptions Negus identifies, held by those in and out of the companies, as well as the tendency to ascribe particular corporate cultures to "gifted or charismatic individuals," explains everything from the mythic status of Rupert Murdoch at News Corp to Mark Zuckerberg at Facebook.

Major record labels are vast organizations, often organized into sub-labels. Negus expands his comparison by assessing the different ways corporate culture impacts in the genres of rap, country, and salsa music to further underscore the "complexity of people, organizations, companies, and alliances, and the historically changing motives, influences, and agendas which shape the production of popular music" (8–9). Negus relies on interviews, and explains how he interprets what his subjects tell him, and triangulates the information in various ways. The result is an uncommonly rich account of a contemporary entertainment industry.

David Hesmondhalgh's research on independent labels and post-punk music contrasts with Negus's major label focus. Hesmondhalgh (1997) examines Rough Trade – a label and more – and its efforts to provide a counter to music industry norms and operate with a more democratic ethos as an act of opposition to the music industry. Through interviews, Hesmondhalgh identifies how Rough Trade was able to develop from a shop, to a label, and a distribution company, and then also create an association of seven regional distributors to provide national distribution for other independent labels. Hesmondhalgh recounts how Rough Trade had a much different standard arrangement from the corporate music industry, offerings musicians 50/50 royalty and album-by-album deals, and recounts the challenges of this attempt to deviate from majors' norms and support a greater diversity of artists and styles.

In another article, Hesmondhalgh (1999) examines two other independent labels – Creation and One Little Indian – to explore how independent labels adopt professionalization strategies from the majors and pursue partnerships. He notes the uncommon construction of indie as a genre characterized by industrial organization rather than music features and that, in this case, indies were best distinguished as labels that attempted a new relationship between commerce and creativity. Hesmondhalgh uses interviews with decision makers at Creation and One Little Indian to develop a deeper understanding of what happened to these labels and their negotiation of creative ideals and commercial imperatives, an account that contrasts with pervasive discourses that tend to frame their fate as one of either selling out or burning out. He also examines the challenges of attributing aesthetics of the music found on these labels to changes in professionalization and industrial partnerships.

Anamik Saha (2011) uses interviews with managers of three independent labels that were part of a popular British Asian electronic dance scene to explore a different set of cultural politics around independent music. Whereas the politics of independence in the post-punk context Hesmondhalgh studies construct independent labels as presenting a challenge or acting in opposition to the music industry, Saha endeavors to explore how the three British Asian independent labels explain their complicated cultural politics relative to postcolonial and racial frames. His interviews reveal the difficulty of evading essentialist constructions of Asian identity and music despite the managers' efforts to be foremost considered as dance labels. Saha uses the responses of his interviewees and the context of British Asian electronic dance music to counter Adorno-ian readings of culture and capitalism and instead as evidence of the "complex, ambivalent, and contested" processes of cultural creation and consumption characteristic of the cultural industries tradition (446). Saha valuably raises the issue of "marginalization through distribution" to explain a consequence of artists choosing to remain with the independent labels for reasons of autonomy and to avoid the semblance of selling out, a decision that also disadvantages them because of the more limited distribution networks of independent labels (448).

None of these accounts of record labels neatly reproduces the norms of study of film studios or newsrooms. Indeed, none of these authors may consider the cited work as an illustration of a media industry study of an organization. Nonetheless, this research clearly sits between the industry and individual level in scale, and its illustration of how the organization – the label – need not be the central object of study is valuable for illustrating the diversity of possible research questions and foci. All of these examples connect questions related to cultural politics with the primary organizations that produce popular music – the majors in the case of Negus and different contexts of independent labels for Hesmondhalgh and Saha.

Conclusion

Although interview research is common at nearly every level, it is important to note the different ways interview research is employed. Notably, interviews are rarely used in the manner of qualitative social science research that aims generalizable results from talking to a sample of respondents. There are some research questions that suit this approach but, within media industry studies, it is far more common to use interviews to elicit particular insight from individuals deliberately selected for their expertise. There is no one right way to use interviews, but researchers should carefully consider their research questions and take the best-suited approach. Qualitative transcription software and analytic tools are often unnecessary when interview subjects are selected purposively, rather than through a sample.

The possible scope of studies at this level is limited only by the imagination of researchers. Although organizations provide a manageable research site, it is crucial that researchers rigorously interrogate what their study adds to broader intellectual conversations. One critique of media industries scholarship is that it has at times over emphasized the case study (Hesmondhalgh, 2010). Rather than indict case-study methodology entirely, we would suggest that researchers have sometimes failed to construct research designs that take a case study of an accessible or interesting site and connect their findings in ways that can extend the body of knowledge of media industry scholarship. All the examples detailed in this chapter avoid this shortcoming, as our explanation of their many contributions identify. Throughout the discussion of different examples in this chapter we have emphasized the larger intellectual questions that different projects have expanded – for example, how Perren's study is not only a detailed account of the Miramax studio in the 1990s, but also points toward structural changes in the larger American movie business during the 1990s. Or in the case of news, how Schlesinger's study of the BBC also provided insight into the practices of newsroom routines more broadly or how Boczkowski's study identified the dilemmas faced by many legacy media industries in the wake of new digital tools. It is also worth keeping in mind that the scholarship we have featured here mobilizes an incredible range of theoretical frameworks.

Where Schlesinger turns to the sociology of knowledge to make sense of BBC newsmen, Boczkowski finds science and technology studies frameworks far more helpful in mapping the interface between technological innovation and organizational structures. Further, Pillai's study of film studios and Saha's account of Brit-Asian record labels remind us that industry studies scholars must be alive to radically different conceptions of culture and value, as well as varied trajectories of capital and labor. Pillai and Saha's work, among that of other scholars, shows clearly that postcolonial studies and critical race theory have much to tell us not only about industries "elsewhere" (non-Western, that is) or independent/ minority media, but also how mainstream media organizations truly struggle to diversify, both in terms of their hiring and work practices *and* what they produce.

Another key point that we hope our array of case studies makes is of the broad value of media industry studies research. Notably, information about organizations is often revealed in many different types of scholarship, including those not explicitly set up as media industry studies. For example, Paddy Scannell and David Cardiff's (1991) social history of the BBC reveals a considerable amount about industry dynamics and organizational operation. And there are many questions and issues that transect media industries. A researcher interested in the BBC should not assume only the works of Born and Schlesinger to be relevant, nor that Boczkowski is more salient than Perren. It is easy to trap one's thinking in a silo of a particular industry and assume that other research on that industry provides the full scope of relevant conversation. Rather, we find searching for research exploring similar types of questions – even if in different industries – productive to grounding scholarship.

In developing organizational-level studies, researchers are well served by thinking broadly about existing questions in the field and how current understanding can be enriched by augmenting established knowledge by investigating adjacent contexts. *Media industry research is often far more valuably categorized by the underlying question than topic.* For example, Hesmondhalgh's and Saha's studies of independent record labels may immediately lead to the classification of this as an expansion of the literature about record labels and, though it does this, it also converses with the questions at the core of Perren's study of "indie" film studios and the complex relationships between forms of popular culture classified as mainstream, and responses to that mainstream. Notably, parallels exist in nearly every media industry. The point here is that knowing a study is about a film studio or a newsroom tells us very little. It is the questions investigated and the theoretical frameworks mobilized – particularly at the individual and organizational levels – that are key to understanding the contribution of the work.

5

Industries and Practices

It may seem redundant or perhaps paradoxical to identify "industries" as a level of analysis in relation to media industry studies. Teasing apart the difference between the *site of study* and *object of the research claim* helps solve this confusion. Scholarship at all the levels explored in this book – despite different sites of study – aims to make research claims about media industries and the consequences of their behavior; perhaps consider this use as capital "I" Industries. In this chapter, we take stock of scholarship that not only seeks answers to questions about Industries, but also engages in research by using the span of a media industry (lowercase "i") as its scale of study. As such, this scope of investigation is broader than the organizations, roles, and individuals, or particular production cultures that we have addressed so far. But it is a crucial step toward a more macro-level approach that brings into view global conglomerates and conditions such as trade agreements that transcend multiple media industries.

Industry-level research explores how different media industries are organized to produce and circulate a specific kind of cultural commodity and the consequences of that industrial organization. This does not imply that scholars incorporate a "soup to nuts" approach that includes every stage of creation and circulation for the industry being studied. Rather, scholars might examine a specific domain of media production and circulation (film distribution, for example), delve into archives to produce a history of a media industry in one particular nation, or examine a specific transition in industry practice that may have precipitated changes in storytelling and representations.

John Thompson's (2013) account of book publishing in the United States and Britain, Todd Gitlin's (1983) examination of 1980s US television, Keith Negus's (1992) pioneering study of popular music production, Yeidy Rivero's (2015) historical account of the formation of Cuban commercial television, and Michael Curtin's 2007 study of the film and television industries in China and Hong Kong are all examples of influential studies that focus on particular media industries. While there are many ways to delimit industry-level studies, scholars do have some tried and tested techniques to imagine and produce both the object of study and the scale of analysis.

Zooming in on a particular region, nation, or city offers one way forward. Connecting with scholarship in cultural geography and anthropology that is concerned with space, place, and the production of culture enriches the context and builds fuller understanding of many major media capitals and regions (Tinic, 2005; Curtin, 2007; Kraidy and Khalil, 2017; Keane, 2015; Straubhaar, 2007; Srinivas, 2013). Another way forward is to examine a particular industry – for instance, a video film industry like Nollywood – while paying attention to its organization and operation across an entire region and at a trans-national scale (Krings and Okome, 2013; Miller, 2012). Some studies, such as Virginia Crisp's (2015) examination of video distribution in the digital age, investigate specific practices that involve examining a broad geographic area. And yet others explore a particular historical moment or track changes in industry practices over time in a specific part of the world. A recent book by Giang Nguyen-Thu (2018) does precisely this by examining the complicated and variable operation of statist and non-statist power in Vietnamese television across different media genres and production contexts. On the whole, this strand of scholarship helps us to understand media industry practices in particular places and times and, in doing so, lays a strong foundation for comparing those practices across geographic contexts, historical periods, and media sectors. Over time, this work helps us discern the many different lines of influence and entanglements (Govil, 2017) that shape media industries worldwide.

The scholarship that we work through in this chapter spans a wide range of industries, tackles a variety of questions, and generates insights into different aspects of the workings of media industries. In the first section, we explore two very different studies of the video-game industry that demonstrate the variation in questions and methods possible when organizing studies to explain industry level behavior.

The second section features scholarship on how phases of industrial change often lead to striking changes in style and aesthetics, storytelling norms, and representations. We first consider a cluster of studies of American commercial television that tie shifts in competitive practices to expansion in representations and stories and then explore scholarship on the production and circulation of television programs when state-run 'national' television industries had to contend with transnational satellite television companies. During the 1990s, a number of countries across the Global South and in the socialist bloc realigned their economies and entered a profoundly uneven global and capitalist world order. In response, scholars in media studies, cultural anthropology, and other cognate fields shifted focus from questions of modernization and development to issues of consumption and cultural politics. These studies of mediated public cultures across Asia, Africa, Latin America, and Eastern Europe include rich accounts of media industry transformations. This body of scholarship is particularly helpful when it comes to understanding the dialectic of globalization and localization in the media industries (Waisbord, 2004; Kumar, 2006) and, crucially, the making of entire new media industry sectors (Tiwary, 2018). More broadly, this line of research provides a crucial foundation for thinking through issues of design, affordances, and the politics of algorithmic curation that we are grappling with today.

In the final section, we focus on studies that examine specific practices of media that are explored at the industry level. For example, how shifts in the marketing practices of the major Hollywood film studios reconfigure the films that are prioritized in development (Wyatt, 1994), how the film exhibition business in the United States adjusted to broader social and economic forces to alter the experience of film going and the market for theatrical release (Gomery, 1992), and how a media industry genders its work and roles (Hill, 2016). Certainly there are many other studies we could draw from. As in other chapters, we select from these in order to construct comparisons and conversations about method and approach.

Expansive Breadth: Cases from Video-Game Industry Studies

A comparison of two books that explore the video-game industries illustrates the breadth of scholarship that can be found at this level. Jesper Juul's *A Casual Revolution* (2010) explores the rise, interest, and playing of video games among people who had not previously played in the first decade of the twenty-first century. The key development that led to this expansion in engagement was the advent of what the industry termed "casual games" or those that are designed to be quickly accessible and that allow greater flexibility in how they are played.

Juul seeks to answer the question "why casual games now?" and does so by illustrating the interplay of multiple factors including the economics of game development and identifying how the lower cost of casual games enabled games to fit into the lives of players differently from core games in a manner that expanded the game-playing audience. As such, the object of Juul's book is the "industry" level, particularly an industrial segment at a specific time: the emergence of the casual game industry as it became financially on a par with the mainstream segment that had defined the industry. Among other questions, Juul asks: "How did casual games appear, and how do they relate to the history of video games and nondigital games?" (22). He partly finds answers by marshaling evidence of a long history of casual games – even if they weren't considered "core" to the industry. The expansion of the marketplace is an obvious strategic move for the game industry, but he also discovers multiple industrial factors including the need for profit-seeking companies to find growth. And there are other simple but crucial forces at work that Juul learns about in his conversations with game developers. The growing interest in casual games can also be attributed in part to game developers for whom increasingly busy lives left little time for hardcore game play.

Notably, Juul's book has a focus that is much broader than the games industry itself. It also incorporates audience/user study and engages in extensive analysis of the games themselves. His contextualized history of casual games and changing industry dynamics – constructed through desk research – exemplifies the type of inquiry that is part of examining an industry, as do his interviews with eleven game developers who do not offer information on their publishers or their role so much as provide insight on the broader context of the industry at the time. The interviews illustrate shifts in thinking and strategies of game developers – and the types of games created – in response to technological changes and the emergence of an audience segment identified as casual gamers.

Juul's interviews reveal that technological changes made game production practices easier, and hardware became better able to support smaller games. He also explores the design and economic factors that allowed low-resolution casual games to emerge at the same moment that industry giants sought to exploit the advancing resolution and fidelity of high-definition games in the core sector. He identifies visual interface as a key force in the rise of casual games because they are "mimetic," or allow the player to mimic the game activity on screen, a factor that makes them more accessible to non-experts.

Further, Juul's use of game-developer interviews helps to avoid a technological determinist argument and reveals the interplay among new technological affordances, cultural factors, and economic priorities of the gaming industry. For example, the developers recalled deriving inspiration from witnessing people engaging in game-play behavior that wasn't characteristic of expectations of play that had guided game production previously: their play was not tied to games that required hours to advance, not played socially, and not tied to home-based consoles. Multifaceted handheld computers – better known as mobile phones – did put game play in the pockets of many more than would commit to the purchase of a console or portable game device, but without intentional development and industrial decisions to create games for these devices and casual contexts, phones might not have become common instruments of game play. Phones – and the games made for play on them – encouraged casual game engagement during breaks in the workday (Tussey, 2018) and expanded perceptions of characteristics of games that could be successful.

Although Juul's book is not designed in the first instance as an industry study, it is a key example of the contextual approach to culture or circuit models that trace a lineage from Stuart Hall's "Encoding/Decoding" (1980) through to Julie D'Acci's (2004) most recent revision of this cultural studies model that advocates for attention to text, production, reception, and context in the exploration of a phenomenon. Juul's book illustrates the value delivered by including dimensions of industry research – particularly an awareness and discussion of the business behind game and console publishing and interviews with game developers – to fully assess the phenomenon of the emergence of casual gaming. Juul interviews game developers, but seeks their insight on "how and why the focus of *the industry* shifted."

Like Juul, Aphra Kerr investigates the video-game industry in *Global Games: Production, Circulation and Policy in the Networked Era* (2017), but takes a much broader view of both games and the video-game industry. Kerr draws from multiple types of evidence to build an explanation and analysis of the contemporary video-game industry. Recognizing the dearth of scholarship about the "digital game industry," Kerr casts a very broad net in defining her object of analysis. Her designation of "digital" games provides some technological and historical narrowing, but she intentionally provides a broad scope. The book is particularly concerned with illustrating and explaining the global character of the digital game industry, a characteristic that distinguishes it from other media industries that operate – or have operated – with the "national" as their imagined terrain. Kerr's examination focuses on "the changing structure of the digital games industry, changing production logics, changing aspects of circulation, and the influences of policy on the global games industry" (11).

Crucially, Kerr begins her analysis by acknowledging the growing complexity of digital game industries – identifying five segments in order to tease apart variation in business models, software production and development, hardware systems, and market concentration. In doing so, Kerr recognizes the difficulty of making industry-level claims or seeking industry-level answers. By first establishing these five segments and their characteristics of differentiation, Kerr is able to explore industry structure, production logics, circulation, and policy on a game *industry* level.

Kerr marshals evidence from a range of sources to make claims about the operation of the video-game industry. Given the scale, much of her evidence comes from global – and occasionally national-level – economic data such as sales revenue of hardware and software, or shifts in the employee corps of different segments of the industry. Such data is helpful in building her case for the global nature of the industry and to illustrate its changing features. Notably, with data derived a few years after Juul's book was published, Kerr illustrates the continued surge of the casual sector, so much so that Tencent – a relatively new player in the games industry focused on mobile gaming – tops the ranking of global revenue, although she also notes all the major companies became more diversified across casual and core games.

In exploring changing production logics, Kerr also draws evidence from interviews with video-game developers. Kerr distinguishes among different production lifecycles (hardware versus software) to explore the nature of work within companies by citing literature focused on labor in the video-game industries, her own interviews, and various trade publications and documentation of industry practices. Both Kerr and Juul provide valuable insight into the operation of video-game industries despite differences in the precise focus of their books, the scope of industry investigated, and evidence used to support their analyses. They are similar, however, in the nature of questions that guide the research and in seeking evidence that might explain a specific sector of the video-game industry (casual gaming) or, at a broader level, mapping the structures of an increasingly global video-game industry.

Several other scholars (Deuze, Martin, and Allen, 2007; O'Donnell, 2014) have interviewed game developers and other game workers to better understand the dynamics of labor in the gaming industry or to explore how organizational norms affect workers and the games that are produced, and are discussed in earlier chapters. T. L. Taylor's pathbreaking work on e-sports (2015) and the rise of game live streaming (2018) points to other gaming arenas, including the growing impact of social media on gaming cultures and the powerful role played by digital platforms like Twitch (owned by Amazon). In *Watch Me Play: Twitch and the Rise of Game Live Streaming*, Taylor draws on interviews with a range of game broadcasters, professionals in e-sports organizations, and first-hand observation of technical, organizational, and production practices at tournament events to examine the "pleasures and work" involved in a broadcasting activity that has engendered new forms of user-generated content and alternative distribution models. With the centrality of video games to global media and digital cultures no longer in dispute, we are sure to see more scholarship on the games industry in the near future. It is also clear that scholarship on the games industry is beginning to address issues of diversity and inequality. For instance, in *Woke Gaming: Digital Challenges to Oppression and Social Injustice*, Kishonna Gray and David Leonard (2018) work with the premise that gaming, like other media and cultural industries, is "entangled with mainstream cultures of systematic exploitation and oppression" (5), and that any account of the games industry has to consider deeply entrenched racial and gendered ideologies that shape the production and dissemination of games across the world.

Connecting Representational and Industrial Change

On the whole, game studies scholarship analyzes the dynamics of industrial change and explores how multiple economic, organizational, socio-cultural, and creative forces shape innovations. Scholars focused on radio, film, and television have also produced such accounts, exploring how changes in core conditions such as ownership (Holt, 2011), technology (Gomery, 2005), or business model (Lotz, 2017) transform the operations of any given media industry. But given that academic interest in the media industries often has been driven by concerns of how industrially produced commodities shape culture and politics, connecting moments of industrial change to shifts in style, aesthetics, and representation has been one of the most vibrant lines of inquiry. Numerous studies of the American television industry in the last few decades provide rich illustrations of how historically grounded studies of industrial conditions help us better understand the emergence of new kinds of representations and, more broadly, the deeply ambivalent relationship between media industries and the cultural politics of race, gender, sexuality, and other forms of identity and difference.

Herman Gray's *Watching Race* (1995) remains one of the most important books in this strand of media industries research. As part of a broader book-length project focused on the shifting meanings of "blackness" on American television, Gray was also interested in understanding the "sudden proliferation of black-oriented situation comedies in the mid-to late 1980s." Given Gray's goal of understanding the "general structures and productive logic of television as a representational system" (xiii), it was clear that textual analysis on its own could not adequately explain representational shifts in popular comedy programs. Understanding the making of race on television would require an examination of structural transformations in the television industry and television's changing role as a cultural institution.

Gray first acknowledges the complex historical, economic, techno-logical, and cultural factors that structured the portrayal of black Americans on US television – a story of near complete erasure that resulted from the mass audience strategy of catering to a predominately white population that undergirded the business from the 1950s up through the 1980s. Gray identifies the beginning of narrowcast strategies at NBC in the 1980s as an important development, as NBC shifted from conceiving of its core audience as one undifferentiated "mass" to instead seek younger and more affluent viewers, even if that translated into a decrease in overall audience size. Drawing from Ken Auletta's (1991) richly detailed book on the takeovers of the broadcast networks in the 1980s, NBC executive Brandon Tartikoff's (1993) autobiography, and trade press articles, Gray argues that a "conscious strategy of going after affluent baby boomers produced noticeable changes in the form, content, and look of programming on NBC in the 1980s" (59).

Gray also connects these industrial forces with broader socio-political changes, and acknowledges that the unprecedented and surprise success of *The Cosby Show* cannot be underestimated. The history of film and television industries worldwide is littered with instances of executives using one breakaway success to begin investing in numerous other films and television programs with similar settings, tropes, and characters. It's no surprise, then, that the success of *The Cosby Show* did lead to several other televisual experiments with black-cast series. What is notable, however, is that many of the series differed considerably from *The Cosby Show* but still proved successful. Gray's research – an early example of analysis of the contemporary television industry within US media studies scholarship – relies primarily on secondary sources and trade press for building an explanation of the structural transformations of the US industry that had been profoundly reorganized by the purchase of the broadcast networks and resulted in their increased corporatization. Gray conducted interviews with producers, writers, and actors, but used that insight more to inform his understanding of the multiple and various ways racialization operated in production contexts than to explain the shifts in network strategy. Gray's work offers a valuable illustration of tying analysis of racial and ethnic representations to industry norms and practices. As Anamik Saha (2018) points out in his book on *Race and the Cultural Industries*, the question of how "cultural industries make race" remained largely neglected and has only been taken up with the resurgence of industry/production studies in the 2000s. Saha's broad view of racialization in the media industries – "a process whereby people and objects and indeed, cultural commodities, come to be inscribed with ideas from race-thinking" (2018, 11) – marks an important intervention. Instead of asking how media industries *represent* race, he examines different industry practices including formatting, packaging, marketing, and diversity initiatives function as sites wherein "ideas about race are actively produced" (11).

This theoretical and methodological shift in thinking about media industries and the politics of cultural representation has also been a concern for scholars examining the operations of the television industries in order to explain the role played by popular programs that tapped into and shaped other vectors of identity and culture.

Ron Becker's *Gay TV and Straight America* (2006) and Amanda D. Lotz's *Redesigning Women: Television after the Network Era* (2006) are two key studies that examine the industrial logics and practices shaping the emergence of gay-themed programming and female-centered dramas respectively. Becker looks for an explanation of the somewhat sudden expansion in gay visibility and gay-themed programming in US primetime television in the 1990s. Notably, like Gray, Becker also first notes a textual phenomenon – that of the surge in lesbian and gay characters and themes – and sets out to find its cause. Becker identifies broader cultural reasons, but also explores the role played by changing industrial practices at the broadcast networks during this period of considerable ferment surrounding queer identity and politics in the United States. In response to an audience marketplace that became increasingly fractured and fragmented as cable channels siphoned away attention – in particular, taking the highly valued attention of younger and more affluent viewers – both network programmers and advertisers reconfigured their assumptions of broadcast television's mass appeal and the corresponding programming (Sender, 2005).

Through analysis of competitive conditions, literature, and data about shifts in the advertising industry, interviews with television creators, and trade press interviews with industry executives, Becker identifies another consequence of the strategy shift of seeking the most 18-to-49-year-old viewers instead of a "mass audience." In fact, Becker develops an analysis of the profound shifts in the business of television since the 1980s that were only dimly perceived by industry insiders and scholars alike at the time. He draws from viewership data to illustrate the shrinking audience reached by any single television outlet despite robust viewership of television on the whole. Incorporating data about commercial spending by advertisers and probing the television industry's strategy as channels sought a narrow segment of audiences, Becker maps the challenges that broadcasters faced. Crucially, he marshals evidence to support the claim that the networks weren't seeking merely to reach gay and lesbian viewers, but that the incorporation of gay themes derived from the value of programming that had a progressive sensibility attractive to certain straight audience members as well. Of course, this seemingly "edgy" programming would only go so far, and relied on well-worn mistaken-sexual-identity plotlines to make sure that "straight panic" would not set in with American audiences at large and, in the process, jeopardize the emergent potential of niche-marketing and segmented TV programming strategies.

In *Redesigning Women: Television After the Network Era* (2006), Lotz further probes the shift from mass audience norms to narrowcast targets to explain the emergence of a preponderance of female-centered dramas on American television during the 1990s. The appearance, and success of a diverse array of series including *Buffy the Vampire Slayer*, *Ally McBeal*, *Providence*, and *Judging Amy* could be tied to broad-casters' waning prioritization of male viewers that increasingly found more targeted offerings on cable channels. Lotz draws from similar industrial data, trade press reporting, and interviews with executives and creatives to understand the profound expansion in dramas with female protagonists, at the same time that a channel branded as "Television for Women" spent twenty-six months as the most-watched cable channel, and two other female-targeted channels launched to compete.

Though related, the root industrial dynamics that gave rise to black situation comedies, gay-themed programming, and female-centered series weren't precisely the same. The three phenomena appear at different times and relate to different aspects of a twenty-year adjustment in industry norms. Becker is able to indicate the importance of gay-themed programming to attracting straight viewers, while Lotz digs into the specific characteristics of women targeted by the industry since "women" can't really be understood as a niche audience. It is worth noting, however, that we do need some historical distance before we can fully grasp the relative influence of different economic, regulatory, political, and cultural forces at work. For instance, in a recent book, *We Now Disrupt This Broadcast: How Cable Transformed Television and the Internet Revolutionized It All* (2018), Lotz was able to explore another aspect of the industrial shifts of the 1990s in an investigation of the industrial forces that led to the development of original scripted series by US cable channels. Lotz identifies the broader competitive forces of the development of DBS satellite service with digital capacity and fidelity and regulatory adjustments initiated by the Telecommunications Act of 1996 as key to instigating a shift in the competitive strategies of cable channels. Original cable series on channels funded by a combination of advertising and subscriber revenue substantially adjusted US viewers' perceptions of the boundaries and characteristics of television programming. Within less than a decade, cable original series went from being denigrated to becoming the pinnacle of industry awards and popular culture attention.

All of these cases point us toward a well-worn scholarly approach, one that involves examining shifts in industry operations and strategies as a way to explain striking changes in media programs and the cultural politics they tap into and shape at specific historical conjunctures. It is worth emphasizing again that scholarship in this vein often brings together close textual analysis, a careful account of the broader socio-historical context, and discourses about audiences and their social and political lives as a way to situate industry practices within broader debates about media and the politics of representation. Drawing on a range of evidence – data about industrial characteristics, firsthand and published interviews with industry executives and creatives, observation of industry conventions and production processes, and analysis of trade publications and other sources in which industry professionals speak to or about their sector – this work has enriched our understanding of the links between industrial change and representational practices.

Charting Structural and Textual Changes

When we explore scholarship on film and television beyond the US and the UK, it becomes clear that industry dynamics are often situated in relation to the cultural politics of nation-states with the emphasis remaining on films and television programs on the one hand and audiences/reception on the other (Mankekar, 1999; Abu-Lughod, 2005). There were notable exceptions, such as William Mazzarella's (2003) ethnography of the advertising industry in Mumbai. However, scholars who analyzed the complex links between economic and cultural globalization by examining sites like satellite television did incorporate rich accounts of industry dynamics and practices even as they focused on programs, audiences, and the politics of cultural hybridity (Kumar, 2006; Fung, 2006; Parks and Kumar, 2002).

Shanti Kumar's (2006) *Gandhi Meets Primetime: Globalization and Nationalism on Indian Television* remains a key study of the transition from statist to commercial television. In this book, Kumar's primary goal is to understand how the entry and establishment of transnational media companies like Star TV and translocal networks such as ZEE and Sun led to new imaginations of the national community during the 1990s. To develop his argument that "the rapid transformations of electronic capitalism in general and the growing competition among television networks in particular have necessitated radical reimaginations of nationalism in postcolonial India" (2), Kumar examines a range of television programs and tracks news and popular discourse surrounding some of the more contentious programs. But a substantial part of his analysis also involves a detailed analysis of policy and regulatory shifts involving the state-run broadcaster (Doordarshan) and debates about public vs. corporate control of India's airwaves. In the first chapter, Kumar traces the changing identity of Doordarshan as a state-sponsored network, the evolution of television during the 1970s, and how shifts in India's political economic structures at large led to the commercialization of the state broadcaster and the move toward sponsored programming.

Kumar's analysis speaks to the fact that a vast majority of nations around the world invested significant resources to develop *national* television industries (Lent, 1978; Abu-Lughod, 2005; Head, 1974; Bai, 2005). As Joseph Straubhaar points out in his survey of world television, these media industries "worked within national markets defined in a reciprocal relationship with government policy and national identity" (2007, 55). Scholarship on the economic, political, and cultural role of nation-states in the era before neo-liberal globalization (1950s to 1980s), the influence of national and state media conglomerates (TV Globo in Brazil, Televisa in Mexico, or CCTV in China), and the role of business and cultural elites in the evolution of media industries across Asia, Africa, and Latin America has been vital for understanding the dynamics of globalization and localization of media industries beginning in the 1990s. We should hasten to add that drawing attention to the role of the state does not imply that television industries and cultures have ever been thoroughly 'national'. As Sabina Mihelj and Simon Huxtable (2018) point out in their account of television in countries under communist rule, national television industries were entangled not only with other socialist states but also "with their counterparts on the other side of the Iron Curtain" (53). Understanding the relations between industry dynamics and textual change thus calls for historical specificity and, crucially, theoretical and methodological frameworks that are able to account for statist, public, and private modes of ownership, organization, and operation.

A recently published doctoral thesis on the cultural history of video in India also speaks to the potential of industry-level research to examine the intersections of technological change, media infrastructures, and the emergence of entire new industry sectors (Tiwary, 2018). Ishita Tiwary begins from a decidedly textual/formal place and identifies four key "genres" as crucial for understanding video culture(s) in India – the marriage video, straight-to-video productions, video news magazines, and religious videos. In the first chapter, Tiwary addresses the emergence of a "cottage industry" with aspiring filmmakers, established photo studios, and a host of media entrepreneurs coming together to produce "marriage videos." Building on key scholarship on film and television genres, Tiwary also explores how this particular arena of media production was shaped in crucial ways by access to new media technologies, such as editing hardware and software, and sound technologies including mixers that would go on to transform television production in the 1990s.

She then narrates the story of straight-to-video productions by focusing on one particular company (Hiba Films). Given that television studies in the Indian context has not delved deeply into industry structures and dynamics, we also do not have a good understanding of the operations of state-run TV during the 1980s and certainly no careful account of the impact of home video on television, or the film industries, for that matter. This analysis offers a much-needed understanding of how video technology created an opportunity for a strikingly new genre of made-for-TV films. Tiwary next explores two other key genres – the news magazine and video productions focused on religious movements. Immensely popular in the years leading up to the 24 x 7 news revolution, video news magazines played a key role in mediating the political for audiences with little choice other than state-run television's (Doordarshan) carefully curated nightly news segments. Here, she also makes a vital contribution to our understanding of journalism in the Indian context and suggests a path forward for media industry scholars interested in exploring forces and factors leading up to the explosion of cable news in the mid to late 1990s. Finally, she examines the creative uses of video in the domain of religious instruction (*pravachan* – sermon or disquisition on a specific religious and moral topic) and focuses on the charismatic Osho Rajneesh (made all the more notorious by Netflix with its hit miniseries *Wild, Wild Country*). Bringing together first-hand accounts of the ashram (the organization of the space, daily activities of the devotees, etc.) with a careful reading of the *video pravachans* that were used to recruit followers to the "cult," this chapter makes a vital contribution to the study of media industries and religion, a decidedly under-examined topic.

Tiwary's project also alerts us to a broader methodological problem in media industries research. In many contexts around the world, media archives – particularly in relation to television and video – are far from organized and in some cases government institutions control the material. In this instance, Tiwary had to rely less on organized archival material and instead construct one herself by gathering a wide range of industry artifacts and primary materials, in-depth interviews with industry professionals (many of whom no longer work in this particular business), and close readings of a carefully selected set of videos. At a broader level, Tiwary's project makes it clear that we now have a wealth of scholarship on media cultures and industries across the world and that this body of work serves as a robust platform for a new generation of scholars to carve out space for studying industries and institutions in more detail and depth.

These links between industry changes and representations are difficult to pinpoint if we take too macro a view. As we will see in the next chapter, it is difficult to connect ownership changes or trade agreements between nations, for instance, to the routine production of television programs or specific programs themselves. And by the same token, an industry-level study will not necessarily reveal the workings of a particular media company (a film studio, for instance) or the production culture of an advertising agency.

Studying Industry-Wide Practices

There are many other questions and topics that can be the focus of an industry-level study. Depending on the existing resources in the field, such studies often must explain and establish the underlying industrial dynamics before analyzing their cultural significance. The final section of this chapter pivots from studies that aim to provide fairly expansive accounts of media industries to those that focus on a particular industry practice. By "industry practice," we mean to single out those specific, identifiable activities in which industries and institutions engage. One can think of practice, in this sense, as including strategies put into action, as well as broad sectors of an industry that are essential to its operation. Such studies are arguably broader than the behavior of particular organizations, but focus on a component of industry operation.

In some cases, studies of industrial practice link also to questions regarding textual change, as discussed above. In *High Concept: Movies and Marketing in Hollywood* (1994), for instance, Justin Wyatt seeks to understand the rise of "high concept" as a major strand of post-classical Hollywood cinema. In doing so, Wyatt details the new and powerful role that marketing and market research wielded over the New Hollywood. As he defines it, high-concept cinema entails a simplification of character and narrative and an integration of the content and style of a film with its marketing, advertising, and soundtrack. Wyatt's interest in textual change is fully intertwined with grasping larger changes in the American movie industry after 1960, including conglomeration, the advent of new technologies like home video and, perhaps most importantly here, "the rise of marketing and merchandising" (18). Thus, this book – like several already discussed – seeks to connect textual, formal change to industrial factors; as Wyatt states: "High concept can be considered as one result of the tension between the economics and aesthetics on which commercial studio filmmaking is based" (15).

Wyatt details the formal tendencies of high-concept cinema before proceeding to chart the historical changes in the structure of Hollywood and the larger market for commercial cinema following World War II. He discusses the conglomeration of the major studios, the rise of home video and cable, and the increasing importance of blockbusters to the Hollywood studios among other phenomena. Yet, in addition to such structural changes, Wyatt notes the pronounced importance of *marketing* to Hollywood during this period, a practice that aimed to distinguish certain characteristics of a film to appeal to different segments of the audience in order to provide product differentiation. Wyatt situates high concept as an especially important form of product differentiation because the popular imagination of these films is so tied to their marketing and, in the process, they "are targeted to a certain audience in conception, thereby making their media campaigns much more specific and directed" (105). To support his argument, Wyatt examines case studies of different films' marketing campaigns, including analyses of print advertisements, examinations of different films' soundtrack albums, as well as merchandising practices from the 1970s onward.

Wyatt concludes with a survey of the history and typical methods of market research. Although Hollywood had engaged in market research for a long time, this practice became standard by the late 1970s. Wyatt offers a statistical model to account for the financial success of a sample of over 500 films released between 1983 and 1986 to test his idea that "high concept films should be the most amenable of any filmmaking to market research" given their simplified narratives and easy marketability (161). Although quantitative research is common in mass communication scholarship, Wyatt's use of statistical analysis was, and remains, highly unusual in humanities-based scholarship on cinema. Wyatt's analysis finds that, indeed, the box office revenues of high concept films were easier to predict than those of other types of films, making high concept attractive to Hollywood because it "lowers the risk and uncertainty within the movie marketplace" (172). Although he refrains from making an argument about causality, Wyatt does argue that "high concept should be interpreted as the product of an industry driven by market research" (174). The book consequently succeeds in explaining a relationship between business practices and textual forms, and moreover, in detailing specific practices that occur on an industry-wide scale, in this case marketing and market research within the film industry.

Where Wyatt provides an industry-scale analysis by looking at how particular business practices such as marketing and market research affected the movie industry and film form, other scholarship examines an entire sector of an industry to conceptualize specific practices. An example of this is Douglas Gomery's *Shared Pleasures* (1992), which provides a study of "movie presentation in the United States" from its beginnings through the early 1990s. Approaching the subject of "presentation," rather than just "exhibition," enables Gomery not only to look at the movie-theater business, but also television, cable, and home video. With the goal of providing a broad-minded historical overview, Gomery focuses on the business and sociological aspects of film presentation; as he states: "Analysis of the economics of exhibition demands more than business history but also a grappling with technological change and social implications" (xviii), and further that: "The economic structure and behavior of an industry often leads to important social change. Such is the case with moviegoing" (xviii).

The book does not follow a perfectly chronological order. Rather, the first third of the book examines "the business history" of movie exhibition in the United States, the middle section looks at "alternative operations" like black theaters and art cinemas, and the final section examines television, cable, and home video. Gomery's work draws from numerous trade publications, newspapers, and popular and specialty magazines; he also makes use of historical and social science scholarship, biographies of prominent figures, and industrial reports. This material supports an analysis that alternates between big-scope claims regarding industrial trends and close-up case studies of specific firms, individuals, or business practices. Not only does Gomery's study demonstrate the interdependence of industrial and technological change, but it is also a good example of an industrial study that broadens out to make claims about cultural change. In this regard, his book provides a complex and nuanced sense of how multiple forces altered the business of movie exhibition over time.

For instance, Gomery connects the rise and changes in American movie presentation – from amusement parks and vaudeville theaters, to nickelodeons, to the opulent "movie palaces" of the 1920s – within the context of changes in the national economy, as well as broader trends within American business at the time. Thus, when charting the rise of the Balaban and Katz theatrical operation in the 1910s to 1920s, Gomery links its expansion to that of Sears-Roebuck, Woolworths, and other retailers at the forefront of "the ongoing chain store revolution" (35). Further, he also shows how Balaban and Katz benefited from the trolley and elevated train system in Chicago to construct a clear picture of this company, but within a larger economic and social context.

Even while *Shared Pleasures* provides a wide-ranging picture of one sector of the film industry, it still attends to some specific industrial players, processes, and practices. Gomery devotes considerable space to looking at theaters that specialized in showing newsreel films in the 1920s to 1940s, for instance, and punctuates this with more detailed histories of specific newsreel chains. Similarly, Gomery discusses HBO and Blockbuster Video within his discussion of cable television and home video, respectively. Just as important, Gomery attends to specific business strategies that characterized the movie presentation business at different moments, whether that meant the invention of "double features," the implementation of air-conditioning in movie theaters, or the ways in which black theaters advertised to potential customers. In this manner, *Shared Pleasures* supports its broad historical account with details regarding some of the specific companies and strategies that shaped the ways that Americans accessed movies during the twentieth century. In turn, this shows how industry-scaled scholarship can still attend to some of the specific companies, business practices, or social and cultural events that shaped an industry.

Although it does not exactly examine a "practice" nor a "sector," Erin Hill's (2016) study of female workers in Hollywood, *Never Done: A History of Women's Work in Media Production*, represents a critical analysis of a single, but defining, aspect of an entire industry. Hill's work charts the historical adjustment of roles held by women within the Hollywood work force as they were pushed into marginalized, low-status – though still essential – roles over time. Hill makes a strong case that the largely invisible administrative labor performed predominantly by women was essential to Hollywood's formation as a modern, complex, multi-faceted enterprise. Yet the very invisibility of female work in Hollywood, either because of outright erasure or through a lack of documentation because women's work was seen as so insignificant, challenges her research practice. Hill is inventive in addressing and overcoming this lack of conventional archive that is a product of the sexism that the book seeks to redress, by drawing on unusual materials like studio maps and studio tour films that inadvertently speak to Hollywood's gendered division of labor, as well as memoirs and other rare instances of women's documentation of their work experiences. Through its focus on female labor in Hollywood and the processes through which it has been marginalized and even rendered invisible, *Never Done* represents an excellent model for conducting industrial studies that critique an entire industry by reading against the historical grain.

Conclusion

The research discussed in this chapter engages a wide range of method-ologies. Much of this scholarship is supported through desk research of industry trade press and industrial histories that are used to advance new knowledge about a shift in industrial practice that led to changes in the media commodities produced as a result. Importantly, many of these publications also contextualize the industrial change within a broader socio-historical or economic context – for example, Becker's attention to legal and political activism around gay rights, or Gomery's accounting for the significant role of suburbanization in changing film-going habits.

Examinations of media industries do not always have to focus on change, but phases of change do serve as rich opportunities for scholars interested in mapping shifts in media industries and because moments of change disrupt norms that otherwise seem unalterable. For example, the use of digital technologies for media production and circulation over the past two decades has had wide-ranging implications for media and cultural production. In *The Music Industry*, Patrik Wikström (2020) attends to the significant reconfiguration of popular recorded music as the selling of music goods has been replaced as a dominant revenue stream by fees paid by streaming services. Such a core adjustment in revenue stream has engendered other changes in the business, ranging from the conditions of contracts labels use to sign artists, to the consequences that easily available, professional recording and production tools have on music-making practices, which in turn affect the everyday lives of musicians and the music they create. Indeed, the fact that Wikström's book has already gone through three editions (first edition in 2010) speaks to the incredible pace of change in the recorded music industry.

And even when research sets out to establish and analyze norms of industrial practice, change can intervene. In his account of the trade book publishing industry, John B. Thompson (2013) endeavors to establish the "logic of the field" of Anglo-American trade book publishing just before digital distribution and the rise of Amazon reconfigured it. His account acknowledges how the emergence of book superstores such as Borders and Barnes and Noble led to a "hardback revolution" through their heavy discounting of popular hardbacks as loss leaders to encourage people into stores, and how that had the effect of eroding the paperback market and diminishing the value of publishers' back catalog that had been a source of steady and reliable yearly income. Thompson builds an elaborate explanation of the interconnections among various agents and organizations that play roles in the creation and circulation of trade books and analyzes how they leverage five forms of capital (human, economic, social, intellectual, and symbolic) in these interactions.

We have sought both to identify commonalities among research at this level as well as the breadth that is possible in a level of study that centers on industries, their practices, and their subsectors. Careful crafting of manageable research questions is crucial to industry-level study because of the potential breadth of the field, even when demarcated to a particular time or place. And as we have indicated in this chapter, one way to make an industry-level study manageable is to begin with a set of media texts or cultural practices.

As the cases explored here illustrate, industry-level studies often provide a sense of how broad forces such as ownership, technological, or sociocultural change can adjust the field of industrial operation. Industry dynamics often structure tendencies in the operation of its component parts and can profoundly contribute to the relative power among different sectors – for example the relationship between the studios and exhibitors in Gomery's book. Industries and their sectors are ultimately agglomerations of other entities – particular theaters, networks, stations, game publishers, and so on. In the previous chapter, we surveyed scholarship on particular organizations in order to explore how media industry studies begins to achieve a better view of the daily conditions and challenges that directly explain common features – and the occasional deviation – in the media commodities produced.

In the next chapter, we take a step back from the daily, on-the-ground workings of media industries and their organization to adopt a macro-level, political-economic, and global perspective. After all, the media industries are part of a world-system involving nation-states, transnational capital flows, and supra-national organizations such as the WTO and UNESCO. The dynamics within and between these and other entities and forces do shape the formation of media markets and the exercise of cultural power in our world today.

6

The Macro View

In October 2001, Robert McChesney sparked a heated debate about global media conglomerates and democracy that captures the importance and complexity of thinking about the political economy within which media industries operate. Writing in *Open Democracy*, McChesney lobbed the first grenade. Taking stock of neoliberal economic policies and new media technologies at the turn of the twenty-first century, McChesney declared that media power had become concentrated and "fewer than ten transnational giants" now controlled the production and circulation of media and information across the world. Liberal democracy, he went on to suggest, was in grave danger in this oligopolistic global media system, unless citizens across the world fought for a vibrant public media sector that would be free from both state and big business interests.

Within a couple of weeks, Benjamin Compaine responded and declared that McChesney's central thesis – that there are fewer large conglomerates controlling the global media system – had no empirical basis. Paying close attention to the range of media companies that operated even within a conglomerate like Viacom and Bertelsmann, Compaine (2001) argued that media consumers had more choice than ever before. The debate soon broadened beyond this narrow focus on media ownership with cultural studies scholar David Hesmondhalgh's nuanced critique. Pointing out that ownership is only one part of the story, Hesmondhalgh outlined how the risky nature of the media business, the agency that professionals in the media industries do wield, and the profoundly contradictory nature of media entertainment and popular culture paints a much more complex picture. Neither complete corporate control nor unfettered free market competition explained the role of media industries in shaping culture and politics (2001).

Hesmondhalgh's nuanced perspective found support as scholars and activists from Hungary, Pakistan, and Japan – contexts different from the Anglosphere – joined the discussion. Ildoko Kaposi (2001) pointed out that Hungary's media system in the post-communist era was shaped not only by American film and television, but also by immensely popular Brazilian and Mexican soap operas. France, Germany, and Britain also wielded influence given long-standing cultural flows between powerful Western European nations and Eastern Europe. Gesturing to scholarship on localization and cultural hybridity that had gained ground in media studies through the 1990s, Kaposi also noted that programs that had been licensed from American media companies, for instance, did well so long as they were carefully and creatively adapted to resonate with decidedly local cultural tastes. Beena Sarwar (2001) added another layer of complexity to this debate by drawing attention to the fact that in the Pakistani context, the government, rather than media conglomerates, was the primary threat to media ownership and diversity of media content.

A few months later, James Curran had the last word (2002). Taking a broader historical and transnational view, Curran pointed out that it was simply too early to make sweeping claims about a global media system. While the dynamic in many industrialized nations was leaning toward increased concentration in the media sector, the global media landscape remained fragmented. Across Europe, Asia, and Latin America, public broadcasting and state-run media organizations were responding creatively to forces of globalization. Indeed, the nation-state remained a key arbiter when it came to re-defining the media industries in an era of accelerated economic and cultural globalization. Curran, a founding member of the Westminster school of media studies in the UK, was offering an important lesson: macro-level perspectives on the media industries are valuable and can reveal global shifts and political-economic patterns, but only if they account for historically distinct modes of cultural production.

We begin with this account of what might seem like a tempest in an academic teapot to signal that the broader question – how do societies maintain the cultural foundations for robust public debates and democratic practices and institutions amid a highly concentrated and capitalist media industry? – remains one of the most important questions for us today, as we contend with the thoroughgoing digitalization of virtually every domain of the media industries. Examining the political economy of media industries provides a powerful theoretical and analytical framework for mapping and understanding the shifting relations between nation-states, media markets, and power relations in varied contexts around the world. As Athique, Parthasarathi, and Srinivas suggest, a macro-view "illuminates the integration of commodities, infrastructure, and the many different types of capital – not just financial, but also natural, human, social, and cultural – at work in the media economy" (2018, 9).

Furthermore, attending to the dynamics of the global political economy does not necessarily mean surveying media industries from the vantage point of a satellite circumnavigating our planet. Rather, it is to signal that we use "political economy" in this chapter to describe the structuring conditions of the playing field upon which media industries exist and operate, and explore how media industries scholarship has studied that foundation. Research at this level engages topics that transcend specific industries, such as movies, games, or music, but considers the broader forces that constrain and enable *what* media industries can do and *how* they function. As the chapter introduction suggests, questions about ownership have been a frequent concern of this scholarship, and as we explore in the rest of the chapter, so too have media imperialism, cultural policy, and research that aims to make cross-industry claims.

Developing theory about the effects of political and economic foundations or their role in shaping media industry behavior has been a tricky task for media industry scholarship. The scale and scope of something so expansive has, at times, led to scholarship that has made overly grand claims. Sometimes, this is just the nature of theory building, particularly when ideas are first developing, based on generalities and without a wide base of evidence. In these cases, we often find that claims of how "media industries" operate do not bear out consistently when grounded in specific studies.

To be clear, there is a distinction to be made between taking a macro-level view of media industries and making *totalizing* claims or theories regarding those industries; the debate regarding media ownership that opened this chapter speaks to this tension. With this caveat in mind, we adopt the perspective of scholars such as Hesmondhalgh (2019), who conceptualize media industries as "complex, ambivalent, and contested." Moreover, we assert that it is possible to hold this presumption of complexity and still engage examination of the underlying political and economic foundations upon which media industries operate.

Features of the political economy as we understand them focus on characteristics of the nation-state, such as whether the media system exists in a democratic or authoritarian context; whether media exist as privately held or publicly traded commercial enterprises, or are supported through funding offered by the government and charged with supporting the public interest. The political economy of a media system is also structured by the regulations that allow or disallow certain ownership structures, types of content, and include trade deals and multinational copyright regimes. In centering this chapter on investigations of this macro scale of the role played by political economy in the operation of media industries, we do not conflate the critical political economy *approach* discussed in detail in Chapter 1. The focus of work in the critical political economy approach is wide ranging – it often considers questions at the macro scale but is also effective for examining dynamics within industries, organizations, and particularly labor dynamics faced by sectors of media workers.

The questions this scale of media industries scholarship wrestles with are broad and multifaceted and make the thematic section organization of other chapters more difficult to construct. Instead, we explore key works that examine the role of political economy in practices of media imperialism and cultural policy as two areas that have been a common focus of scholarship. We deliberately identify examples of scholarship that explore the influence of the features of the political economy in grounded and specific cases, at times juxtaposing such approaches with scholarship that takes a more general approach.

Notably, the repetitive methods used for researching the political economy of media can be difficult to discern. Most research relies on document and data analysis. One of the most challenging features of this work can be gaining access to the data needed, or even the existence and public availability of data. We also select cases that allow us to illustrate the different insights that can be gained depending on what data is used. For example, for a long time, a key data point about the global circulation of television focused on aggregate import and export data. Research by Joseph Straubhaar (2007) offered valuable refinement of that analysis by also examining when imported television shows were scheduled. Straubhaar found that often, US imports were used to fill out schedules in overnight and less viewed periods. This helped make clear the importance of locally produced television despite what country-level import data suggested.

We conclude the chapter by turning to scholarship that focuses on the structuring role of economic practices outside of nation-states and current debates about the digitalization of media production and circulation and the role examining the underlying political economy might play in answering some of the pressing questions they have introduced. The political economy of media, whether ownership and corporate organization or state policies regarding trade or labor, does indeed structure logics of industries, production practices, and the people who work within them, but they are not completely determinant. Negotiation, co-optation, deviation, and even resistance are part and parcel of the operations of the media industries the world over (Hesmondhalgh, 2019). Overall, we would argue that it is possible and necessary to keep the macro-scale – of nation-states and global capitalism – in our view while training our focus on different domains and levels of media industries.

Explaining Media Imperialism

If questions about how societies might support political debate and democratic practices and institutions amid a concentrated and capitalist media industry is the basis for scholarship trying to explain how ownership shapes the operation of media industries, then understanding the imbalanced relations among different nation-states and their media is a central question for research on media imperialism. Questions of state power, commercial media systems, and cultural hegemony have been constant for media industry research from its earliest days – as recounted in Chapter 1. Many of these questions are first raised in the scholarship of Herbert Schiller and Dallas Smythe, who examined and theorized the power of transnational media and communication companies, beginning in the 1960s. Schiller's work offered a model for situating media companies in relation to other businesses, state policy, and geo-political relations. In addition to examining the growing influence of corporate media on social, political, and economic life in the United States and other developed nations, Schiller developed an international perspective to show how the same powerful media interests shored up America's imperial position in the world. *Mass Communications and American Empire* (1969) remains a key text in this regard.

In this book, Schiller traced how the United States had come to replace European powers (UK, Germany, and France) as the world's center of capitalist, military, and communications power in the post-World War II period. Situating the emergence of American power in relation to the Soviet Union and the development of newly independent nation-states across the world, Schiller examined how the American empire was premised on the spread of an inter-linked set of forces: a capitalist economy, liberal democracy, and consumer culture. For Schiller, the spread of this model from the American "center" to the Soviet bloc and outwards to peripheries of the Third World relied on "cultural imperialism," which he later defined as "the sum processes by which a society is brought into the modern [US-centered] world system and how its dominating stratum is attracted, pressured, forced, and sometimes bribed into shaping social institutions to correspond with, or even promote, the values and structures of the dominating centres of the system" (Schiller, 1976: 9).

Beginning with this broad claim, Schiller went on to focus on the centrality of media and communications to forge links across three areas of American imperial power – economic, geopolitical, and cultural. Schiller approached American media and communications companies in relation to other business sectors and, in doing so, showed how media industries had become major economic players both domestically and internationally. He argued that "American interest in overseas communications" extended "from direct ownership of broadcast facilities" to "equipment sales, management service contracts, and program exports" (Schiller, 1992, 125). American media companies, in Schiller's view, did nothing less than bring an entire "infrastructure of socialization" (1976, 9) to bear on the developing world. And what is more, Schiller argued, deep involvements in the media and communications sector enabled further capital investments and other, non-communications related American corporations to establish themselves in foreign markets.

In Schiller's analysis, this market-driven "cultural imperialism" needed the support of the American state and policy apparatus, and he accounted for the role of the American state in supporting the interests of commercial media power both within the United States and abroad. For instance, the US State Department routinely invoked the "free flow of information" doctrine to force nation-states to open their markets to American media conglomerates. Finally, Schiller drew links between the global circulation of commercially produced media and American efforts in propaganda and public diplomacy, such as Radio Free Europe and Voice of America. He argued that American media did not just lure audiences around the world into admiring the American way of life, but that the asymmetric flows of media from the United States to the rest of the world effectively secured consent for American foreign policy as well.

Schiller used national data, such as import and export information, as the basis of his explanation of the patterns of global media flows. As we've addressed, he grounded his theory of American corporate behavior in particular practices. On the whole, Schiller's work on media and American cultural imperialism forced scholars in media and communication studies to take seriously the profoundly asymmetric power relationships between US communications and media companies and those in poorly resourced developing nations, even if the situation varied country to country. His focus on these foundational conditions led him to propose a core-periphery model for understanding the global media landscape, and offered a framework for scholars examining Latin American, Asian, and other postcolonial contexts to move beyond issues of modernization and development to focus on relations between the state, media industries, and institutions, and cultural policy. Schiller's work was supported by other scholars including Armand Mattelart (1976; 1979), who addressed the specific forms of US media and cultural imperialism in Latin America.

But the evidence Schiller and other scholars drew from only told part of the story. While the industrial and ideological goals he notes may have encouraged the model he suggested, the actual functioning of industries, organizations, and individuals did not always follow this script. As Joseph Straubhaar (1991) pointed out in an important critique of media imperialism theories, dependency is rarely imposed on an entire nation, let alone a diverse world region like Latin America, in a neat and uncontested fashion. Drawing on institutional and audience research in Brazil, Straubhaar pointed to a wider range of "interdependencies," wherein "countries find themselves unequal but possessing variable degrees of power and initiative in politics, economics, and culture" (39). Using TV Globo in Brazil and television production in other Latin American contexts, Straubhaar presented a complex model of "asymmetric interdependence" that involved accounting for "interests of domestic and transnational elites, entrepreneurial competition, the agendas and actions of key production personnel, and the effects of state intervention, particularly as policy-maker, provider of infrastructure, and advertiser" (43).

In fact, Straubhaar's work followed several other astute pieces of scholarship that had argued for greater nuance in our understanding of media industries and cultural power. For example, researchers studying Latin American communication began to analyze the phenomenal growth of mass media and commercial television in particular as a cultural terrain that was linked to economic and political domination. In a richly detailed article on "the Mexican formula," John Sinclair (1986) draws on Fernando Cardoso's (1977) formulation of dependency to explore how a three-way relationship involving the Mexican bourgeoisie, their ties to transnational corporations and circuits of capital, and the Mexican state, shaped the development of commercial television. US imperialism, in other words, was a poor explanation for the operations of monopoly corporations like Televisa. Sinclair's arguments are not based on primary research, either archival or field study, but on a close reading and historical contextualization of Spanish-language reports, trade and news articles, and a handful of studies and analyses published by Fondo de Cultura Economica, an influential non-profit publishing group. It is impossible to overstate the importance of gathering and reading news, trade publications, policy and government reports, and scholarship in various local languages when trying to understand the political economy of a nation's media sector.

The influence of media imperialism and dependency theories also extended beyond the US–Latin American sphere. In the UK, Philip Elliot and Peter Golding (1974) and Rita Cruise O'Brien (1979) explored asymmetries in the international flow of news and entertainment programming by focusing on Britain and a range of developing nations. These scholars explored how Western media institutions such as the BBC shaped the development of media industries in various African contexts, noting that institutional forms of broadcasting found in the majority of developing countries reflected the state-driven and public service broadcasting models in Europe (Cruise O'Brien, 1975, 92). Moving beyond a focus on ownership and imbalances in the flow of films or television programs, Cruise O'Brien argued that institutional dynamics such as pricing, technical standards, notions of professional expertise and training programs offered by Western media companies (say in France or Britain), and other factors to do with the operations of media industries were also powerful forces of influence. These arguments are based on a careful reading of influential policy reports such as UNESCO's assessment of the sources of imported TV programs and how television programs were being sold (Varis, 1973), and also on interviews that Cruise O'Brien conducted both with key industry professionals, including the Director of Personnel and Training at the main broadcasting corporation in Algeria, and bureaucrats at the Centre for Educational Development Overseas (London), who oversaw the introduction of television services in the Middle East and Africa.

Looking back again, forty-five years later, Cruise O'Brien's work offers a grounded and specific analysis of the dynamics that pressure television importation. Such studies set the stage for more detailed and nuanced analysis of the media industries as the limits of broad theories became clear. Indeed, although the scholarship on media imperialism has consistently examined the role that media industries play in creating and perpetuating imbalanced relations among different nations around the world, this work has been quite varied in the concreteness and specificity of its claims. Further, the scholarship on media imperialism has drawn from an array of different research materials, but is consistent in its interest in uncovering and critiquing the forces that animate the international circulation of media as well as the media's powerful role in shaping global discrepancies in cultural power.

Nation-States, Media Markets, and Cultural Power

Cultural policy plays a crucial role in shaping the political economy of media at multiple scales, from the local, to the national, to the global, and some scholars have examined how such policies are created and deployed in different moments, cultural contexts, and media industries. At the same time, cultural policy represents only one of the complex factors that shape industry activity, forcing scholars to examine policy and policy makers in relation to a range of other constituencies and forces. Manjunath Pendakur's (1985) research, for example, shows how relations between media industries in India and the United States were shaped by state officials, industry professionals, and policy makers acting with varying ideological goals and agendas. To grasp the complex dynamics at work, Pendakur focused attention on the Motion Picture Export Association of America (MPEAA) and its activities.

Beginning with an overview of the formation of the MPEAA, Pendakur first shows how US film companies entered into joint agreements to form a cartel for overseas distribution. He found that how well the MPEAA accomplished its goal of opening up new markets and consolidating established overseas territories in the hands of its member companies depended on the specific country in question. He cross references trade reports published in magazines like *Variety* that provide distribution data over a period of time with trade treaties that document the establishment of state trading corporations to construct a fuller understanding. When read alongside policy reports produced by the Ministry of Information and Broadcasting (such as the "Report of the Working Group on National Film Policy" 1980), trade treaties shed light on how the Indian state used agencies like the *National Film Development Corporation* to try to wrest control over film imports and distribution. To understand the American side of the story, Pendakur relies not only on news and trade sources that are publicly available but also draws on memos written by executives at companies like United Artists to reveal competition between British and US imports during the colonial era to provide a deeper historical context for understanding India's film import policy. (Notably, Pendakur draws from the same archive of United Artists documents as Tino Balio used for his books on the company, as described in Chapter 4.) Further, Pendakur analyzes US state department records, obtained through Freedom of Information Act requests, to show how film distribution dynamics were also shaped by the MPEAA leveraging the political and diplomatic channels through the US embassy and the State department. In these ways, Pendakur shows how policy was formulated amid a complex set of political and economic circumstances.

Throughout, Pendakur shows that even the best efforts on the part of the Indian government and various agencies to establish some reciprocity in film trade were, in the end, rebuffed by the MPEAA. Though the Indian government did manage to extract some concessions from Hollywood, there were broader shifts underway in other media and communications sectors that would complicate cultural policy making. Pendakur's carefully historicized account of India–US film trade ends by pointing to the ways in which forces of economic globalization were already leading to major changes in the media industries in India and other developing nations. Grounded accounts, such as Pendakur's, provide a foundation for making cultural policy responsive to complex and particular dynamics.

However, policy making remains difficult because even when the goal is clear, there are often unintended consequences. In their book *Global Hollywood* (2001), Toby Miller, Nitin Govil, John McMurria, and Richard Maxwell blend critical political economy with cultural studies approaches to explain Hollywood's persistent international success in a book that in many ways extends the analysis and findings of Thomas Guback's study (1969) of Hollywood's impact on the national film industries in different Europen countries after World War II. In *Global Hollywood*, the authors similarly explore evidence of the effectivity of various national and international policy measures in supporting different European cinema industries. The authors' highly critical, even polemical position differentiates *Global Hollywood* from Anne Jäckel's more descriptive overview (2003) of national and multi-national policies regarding European cinema.

Miller et al. assert, broadly, that European cultural policy designed to improve competition with Hollywood through co-productions actually enabled Hollywood to make use of state funds. The authors' analysis of treaties and pan-European co-production funds shows that far from subsidizing and supporting local film productions and cultural labor, poorly resourced initiatives like the European Union's MEDIA programme or the Council of Europe's *Eurimages* scheme were up against European-financed Hollywood films. Though well-intentioned, these initiatives were undercut by national tax incentives that saw, for instance, capital flows of $150 million into the Dutch media sector (93). Further, schemes like *Eurimages* also came laden with other regulatory weights to "promote European character" and to "promote the European film industry" (90). Miller and his co-authors delve into the policy details to show how such schemes privilege bureaucratic elites and their very particular cultural preferences and neglect the plight of below-the-line cultural workers. *Global Hollywood* shows that when "culture" is narrowly defined in terms of above-the-line creative labor, a Hollywood blockbuster like *The Fifth Element* ends up scoring points simply because a French film director was involved.

The focus on policy allows *Global Hollywood* to offer a critical alternative to Hollywood's own explanations for its international success.

The authors ask, if we set aside the industry's self-serving rhetoric about superior content, the universal appeal of its films, and free-market nostrums about meeting consumer and market demands, what explains Hollywood's global power? The answer: Hollywood's command of the New International Division of Cultural Labor (NICL). Steering clear of narratives of cultural homogenization and, at the other end, celebrations of local difference, the authors develop a macro-level explanation that situates Hollywood within a post-Fordist terrain of political and economic structures that emerged in the 1970s (Harvey, 1990). Specifically, Miller et al. locate Hollywood as part of a new era of capitalist development in which low-wage developing countries emerged as key sites for manufacturing goods that were subsequently distributed and sold across the world. Offering a historical account of trade agreements and the power that transnational corporations wielded in this new spatial order, the authors argue that the NICL accounts for the specificities of *cultural* labor, the globalization of labor processes within the media industries, the role played by nation-states in these processes, and crucially, the "means by which Hollywood coordinates and defends its authority over cultural labor markets" (52). Clarifying that NICL is uneven and depends on a range of variables including currency exchange rates, geo-political ties, the strengths and weaknesses of labor movements in various nations, among other factors, the authors identify a set of industry practices to illustrate how NICL operates: co-productions, copyright and intellectual property regimes, distribution and marketing, and audience imaginaries.

Global Hollywood assembles data from various industry, trade, policy, and state sources, and focuses on shifting relations between the state, capital, and the media industries. In the chapter on co-productions, for example, Miller et al. draw on data on co-productions compiled from trade sources such as *Screen Digest* (see Table 3.1 in that work, for example) as well as official policy documents that provide details on cultural policy goals and mandates, incentive structures (write-offs, tax deductions, etc.), labor relations, and at a broader level, national and regional desires and anxieties in relation to American cultural, political, and economic power. There is a genuinely global orientation in that the case studies and examples deployed in different chapters range across the world. Further, while the analysis is based on macro-level trends and patterns, the identification of a set of industry practices – co-production, distribution, marketing, exhibition, and so on – provides an important foundation for other scholars to conduct more in-depth research within and across varied national and regional settings.

But the idea of the NICL is not without limits, many of which result from centering Hollywood as the pre-given national/global frame of reference. To overcome this, Nitin Govil's *Orienting Hollywood* (2015) illustrates how inter-disciplinary scholarship can offer a model for a study that takes a macro-view – a century of film culture and industry encounters between Hollywood and the Bombay film industry – while offering fine-grained readings of images, films, and state and industry discourse. Arguing forcefully for a transhistorical and comparative approach, Govil encourages us to not take "industry" for granted and instead to ask how and to what ends the contours of any given media industry are defined at different points in time. Tracing the contested history of Bombay cinema's status as an "industry" allows us to better understand the shifting relations between nation-states and the media industries. Making it clear that we need to be attuned to the production of scales – the politics of media industries claiming the "national" or "global" as their scale(s) of operations – Govil builds on theoretical developments in Inter-Asian studies to craft a comparative approach that refuses a "central, ideal reference point" (33) and instead, mobilizes entanglement and multiple points of references as both method and practice.

The challenge with such a project, of course, lies with working out which industry practices and sites to examine. Informed by deep archival research and a careful reading of news and trade press coverage of the contemporary Hollywood/Bollywood interactions, Govil first identifies a set of problematics that illuminate the dynamics of "comprehension and comparison" (35) between these media industries. For instance, he settles on the broad question of the "copy" and specifically on intellectual property regimes and Bollywood's "remake culture" as practices through which to understand the production of difference in the global media economy. Through a close analysis of *Kaante* (*Thorns*, 2002), a Bollywood film that Hollywood regarded as an "unauthorized" rehash of Quentin Tarantino's *Reservoir Dogs*, Govil shows how *Kaante* actually builds on other Hollywood films to "flesh out the skeletal narrative economy of *Reservoir Dogs*" (72). Alongside other sections on piracy and naming of media industries ('Bollywood', 'Nollywood', etc.), this analysis shows us how the "copy" has broader implications. Dominant understandings of the copy as "inherently inauthentic" (74) sets up a system of comparison whereby emergent industries in the East are seen to secure cultural and economic influence only by copying those in the West. Media industry hierarchies, in other words, are made manifest in textual practices as much as through divisions of cultural labor.

Subsequent chapters tackle issues of finance (co-production and outsourcing), exhibition, labor, and celebrity culture. Throughout, Govil also keeps in focus issues of subjectivity, identity, and affect. Attuned to critiques of global political economy and the turn to understanding "affective labor" by theorists like Michael Hardt and Antonio Negri (2004), Govil devotes a chapter to the social worlds of American and Indian labor in the film industries. Arguing that it is possible to "engage equally with structure, discourse, and practice" (9), he analyzes how entrenched ways of knowing the "other" and discourses of race, religion, class, and national difference continue to shape encounters between LA and Bombay.

Given the range of topics in play, Govil draws on a wide range of sources including policy documents, industry sources, in-depth interviews with industry professionals, archival documents and memos, and fan letters. Govil's study richly demonstrates how scholars can make macro-level claims about histories of media industries (across a century!) while being attentive to different levels of industry operation. Juxtaposing a close reading of films with analyses of state policy, or setting fan letters with details about cinema halls alongside the history of America's influence on India's exhibition infrastructure, Govil shows us precisely how we can work in the gaps between established disciplines and methodological approaches.

As these cases suggest, there are many different sources of information that can be used to explore how the policies of nation-states and other governing bodies affect the operation of media industries. These cases also provide different strategies for examining underlying structures of political economy while still generating analysis that accounts for and addresses cultural particularity.

Underlying Economic Features of Cultural Production

Although the works discussed in this chapter are varied in terms of their argument and mode of analysis, all are deeply concerned with large, macro-scale phenomena that shape the operation of media industries or, alternatively, in how media industries participate in the larger political economy that organizes national and international relations. In a number of cases, we see that scholars have been especially interested in the ways in which media industries interact with state powers and policies as well as the interests of private enterprise. Whether thinking about "cultural imperialism" and imbalances in cultural and political power, looking at how different governments and media institutions shape the international flow of media, or how cultural policy impacts – or fails to impact – relations among different media industry players, much of the media industries scholarship operating at the macro scale offers a critical appraisal of the status quo political economy of media.

Still others, like the French sociologist Bernard Miège (1987), are more interested in assessing how different media industries employ particular business models that significantly shape how media is made, circulated, and consumed. Although there is a body of media economics that examines such questions without emphasizing matters of culture, scholars such as Miège have analyzed the cultural implications of economic features or sought to explain how characteristics of business practice structure media as cultural producers. Miège (1987) creates different categories of media industries – flow, written press, and publishing – in order to make claims grounded in characteristics bigger than particular industries, yet not encompassing all media industries. For example, his category of "editorial model" industries include all those that make one-off cultural commodities such as films, books, video games, and albums. Miège identifies how there is a common industrial logic to this form of goods production that differentiates these media from those produced more continuously, such as newspapers or the operation of radio stations. By exploring the practices specific to industries with this type of logic, he is able to tie features of the economic foundation of media industries to behaviors for sectors of media goods broader than a particular industry.

Miège is thus able to survey the impact of changes across media sectors – direct broadcast satellite, cable, commercialization of local radio, and videotex – by focusing on production and labor processes. Suggesting that the developments are far more complicated than any theories of "media concentration" could account for, Miège goes on to identify the heterogeneous and often clashing "social logics" at work in the publishing, broadcasting, live entertainment, and electronic information sectors. The logic of "flow" in broadcasting – the production and supply of uninterrupted programming – not only gives rise to a particular kind of production culture but also to shifting relations between producers and distributors. Miège points out that the logics that govern the production and circulation of audiovisual commodities depend on the role of the state and whether or not the commodities are consumed and regarded as "public" or "private" goods. In the rest of the article, Miège details the logics at work in other media sectors before arguing that the situation in France cannot be understood as one of "unification under the aegis of multimedia corporations" (1987, 284). Rather, it is the "interweaving" and "differential weighting" of production logics and labor processes across distinct media industries that were likely to determine the structure and operations of the media industries.

More recently, Miège (2011) offered a typology of different modes of reproducibility that distinguish different sectors of – as he terms them – cultural industries. Again, Miège reorganizes media into categories broader than a particular industry and based on material characteristics; in this case, the different relationships between "cultural merchandise"

– or the goods media industries create, and practices of industrial production. The mode of thinking that Miège embraces is simultaneously grounded and not siloed within particular industries and offers useful tools for conceptualizing cross-industry analysis. Whether in his earlier models of media production or this more recent typology, Miège's approach serves to "make strange" – in the language of Russian formalism – attributes that often seem natural and inherent in particular media goods. By instead centering material practices of work and industrial behaviors, Miège exposes commonality among assumed distinct media and contradictions within those apparently rooted in a commonality.

Miège's work in these essays illustrates another approach to grounding theory building with a scope larger than the scale of a particular media industry. Unlike many cases of scholarship that examine media industries at the macro-level, Miège is less interested in state power and official policy but rather in business models and logics. Miège's efforts to theorize different types of industry behaviors helps to create a foundation for cross-media industry comparison that has been infrequent in media industry scholarship.

Conclusion

Over the past two decades, as scholars have mapped the history, formation, and operations of film, video, and television industries in numerous contexts worldwide, the limitations of macro-level theorizing based only on features of national or global political economy have been rendered in stark relief. Indeed, as we have pointed out in the preceding chapters, the spate of PhD dissertations and books about various media industries around the world that developed during the first decade of this century point to two major scholarly shifts: first, a synthetic and integrated approach to media in which the study of industries could be carried out while remaining attuned to concerns about audiences and programs; and second, a more nuanced theoretical perspective on structure and agency that allowed for a focus on different levels – an entire industry, a particular studio, or even a specific group of cultural workers – while accounting for the logics of global capital.

Factors such as ownership are certainly important for identifying general tendencies but it is very difficult to establish reliably predictive theory about industrial behavior and textual outcomes from the macro-scale alone. Moreover, describing ownership structures and tracking change is but one approach (Bagdikain, 2004; McChesney, 1997). There is now a significant body of scholarship that explores factors of market performance and incorporates detailed economic data about industries to better understand their decisions and behavior (Compaine, 1982; Compaine and Gomery, 2000; Athique et al., 2018). Put simply, the question of "who owns what" reveals relatively little information, but it provides a place to start from. A largely overlooked factor of ownership in much media industry study is that of the type of ownership, such as private, publicly traded, foundation/charitable or not-for-profit, or employee ownership. Even here, scholars have been unable to assert that particular types of ownership yield consistent outcomes, but it is another dynamic to be considered in analysis (Picard and van Weezel, 2008).

Studies at the macro level can be helpful in building initial frameworks of understanding and it is clear that the ongoing digitalization of cultures and economies worldwide calls for re-assessments of media and cultural power. Although boundaries of media industries have grown blurry alongside various internet-based forms of communication, the tools that have been used to study the political economy of media are also beneficial to making sense of social media companies such as Facebook and YouTube, search companies such as Google, and companies such as Amazon and Apple that include media production and distribution with core businesses in online retail and device manufacturing. Tax structures, multinational capital flows, regulatory jurisdictions over corporate behavior and market definitions, and other political and economic factors are at the core of establishing grounded understandings of the role of global companies that increasingly play as significant a role in culture as media. But, as in the case of questions of media ownership, sophisticated and nuanced conceptualization of how features of political economy affect the operation and strategies of these companies is needed. Thus, even as we examine the formation of new spheres of economic, political, and socio-cultural domination (be it American or Chinese) in varied geographic contexts, questions about audiences/users, labor conditions in the digital sectors, the dynamics of creator culture on platforms like YouTube as opposed to portals like Netflix, and so on require multiple levels of analysis and theory-building.

Conclusion: Future Directions for Media Industry Studies

At the turn of the millennium, three forces shaped media culture to a significant degree: new digital technologies including the internet, globalization, and government deregulation that led to corporate consolidation of media industries. Discussion of "convergence" became *en vogue* and could encompass aspects of all three of these forces. Although two decades of scholarship have developed since, our understanding of these subjects and the enduring influence of this scholarship remains less certain and in process. These topics continue to be among key areas of academic debate and development, and this concluding chapter points to some emergent areas of inquiry as well as ongoing questions for media industry studies.

Internet Distribution

Notably, all three issues transcend particular media industries and support the expansive and connected approach that drives this book. The consequences of and response to internet distribution have been different for various industries, but it is notable that the issues of the moment enable and even encourage accounts that send us out of specialized industries for insight and inspiration. Moreover, from an industrial perspective, it is also clear that we cannot think in terms of distinct "old" and "new" media industries. The distribution of texts, images, sounds, and video over the internet has created a few new companies and several new ways of communicating, but also introduced tools of communication and information that benefit virtually every industry. Media companies have endeavored upon expansive innovation to diversify their distribution technologies, which has in turn enabled or required substantial adjustments in industrial practices. New digital technologies and the infrastructures of internet distribution have broadened relevant areas of concern for media industry scholars, who increasingly focus more on the infrastructure, devices, and software that enable contemporary media experiences than was characteristic of pre-digital media industry studies.

Scholarship examining the implications of digital technology for media industries has taken many forms – as several of the studies cited in previous chapters suggest. It has investigated the power exerted by companies that distribute words, pictures, and video that now rank among those with the largest global market capitalization and how those companies are able to exert power over governments, each other, and consumer behavior. It has explored industry-level reconfiguration, as new distributors such as Netflix and Spotify have altered the logics of industrial fields in crucial ways. It has probed how specific organizations, such as newsrooms, have adapted to two decades of nearly constant change in how they fund their enterprises and adjusted the news product they produce in response; it has considered how particular roles, such as the daily tasks of journalists have evolved; and it has examined the role influencers play in new advertising economies. Others yet have looked at these topics with a focus on production cultures created by digital technology and media.

A notable evolution of the last decade is the blurring boundary between television and film and the increasing utility of the less medium-specific term of video. Much recent work has broken down the artificial boundary assumed to exist between "new" or "digital" media and legacy television and film. In the last few years, important projects about the creators of social media entertainment (Cunningham and Craig, 2019) and the internet broadcast of e-sports (Taylor, 2018) have blended industrial and cultural analysis in response to the expanding video worlds audiences access. Such research is broadening the necessary sites of study, as developing a holistic account of these industries requires examining intermediaries like technology developers, content moderators, and algorithm designers. Some new sites of activity challenge conventional boundaries of media industry research, as some video-game players and video creators evolve hobbies and amateur leisure activities into professional enterprises run out of their homes. The scale of production activity – from videos to podcasts to musicians posting on SoundCloud and Bandcamp – makes designing systematic study difficult.

What is a representative case? What are common concerns? How can we map the vast array of media production that now takes place outside of recognizable corporate entities that have publicly reported revenue? Furthermore, the turn to digital technologies has prompted a growing number of scholars to examine forms of circulation that lie outside conventional, legally sanctioned industrial structures and to explore the logics and practices of 'informal' media production and circulation (Lobato, 2012; Lobato and Thomas, 2015; Eckstein and Schwarz, 2014). In the case of Nigerian video film or the proliferation of small-scale music and video industries in cities like New Delhi (Sundaram, 2009), this scholarship illustrates how informal modes of production and distribution can be drivers of broader processes of social and economic change. Pirate networks and informal economies reveal new models of media production and circulation and, in the process, often force trans-formations in mainstream media industries. Studies of informal media economies also shed light on audience practices that challenge both industry and scholarly assumptions and narratives about taste, culture, and identity. At a broad level, these sites challenge conventional defini-tions and boundaries of the media industries and encourage us to reflect on the limits of media industries' power to shape cultures.

Of course, there remain many more questions about digital technol-ogies and media industries to ask and answer. The fleeting, evolving, and endlessly iterative nature of digital technologies often means that contexts of study evolve significantly even before a study is complete, and especially before publication. One of the most challenging tasks of working on topics of the contemporary environment is tying them to broader and persistent knowledge building. A lot of scholarship to date has aimed to provide a basic starting point of understanding. Much deeper theorization that builds from the growing range of case contexts is needed, particularly as features of adjusted industry logics begin to stabilize.

Globalization and Media Convergence

For well over three decades now, academics, journalists, artists, and media producers have reflected on the many interconnected economic, political, and socio-cultural dimensions of globalization. While approaches and vocabulary differ, there is a general consensus that the term globalization is indicative of a world in which human life and activity is less constrained by geography. And where the media industries are concerned, it is worth noting at the outset that media globalization is by no means solely a "Western" phenomenon. Beginning in the 1980s, the media landscape across Asia, Africa, Latin America, and the Middle East was altered dramatically as transnational and regional television networks displaced and, in some cases, reinvigorated centralized, public, and often state-regulated media systems. This process has only intensified in recent years as digital distribution and online-video networks (both legal and extra-legal) have expanded their footprints and created new circuits for the flow of media content that crisscross national, linguistic, and other political and cultural borders.

Furthermore, since the early 1990s, a number of cities and regional hubs across the non-Western world – Hong Kong, Chengdu, Mumbai, Bangalore, Accra, Lagos, and so on – have emerged as important nodes in a trans-national network of media and ICT (information and communication technology) design, production, and circulation. In rich accounts of media industries (Curtin, 2003; Govil, 2015) and digital cultures (Chan, 2013), scholars have shown how media and tech capitals emerge through a complex interaction of local, regional, global, as well as national forces and factors. These factors include state policy, technological advances, the built environment, talent migration, and the desires and ambitions of media moguls and venture capitalists. Far from leading to a homogenized world system in which Anglo-American media, culture, and values overwhelm local culture(s) everywhere, the globalization of media has given rise to new and highly hybrid scales and forms of cultural production and cultural identity.

To be sure, these transformations in the media sector were part of broader transitions involving the adoption of neo-liberal economic policies and the de-regulation and privatization of different sectors of the economy. And in many nations, the turn to market-oriented reforms and emergence of commercial media systems went hand-in-hand with new forms of religious nationalism and other reactionary movements (Fernandes, 2006; Abu-Lughod, 2005). But, on the whole, we can see now that in remaking the link between place and culture, globalization has led to proliferation rather than a destruction of media cultures across the world (Tomlinson, 1999).

Scholars including Curtin (2009) were right to point out that the history of media industries research remained focused on film and television in the United States. And where scholars looked beyond the United States, they have been concerned primarily with issues of media/cultural imperialism, national policy, and aesthetics (Curtin, 2009). A decade hence, our own assessment points to a richer body of scholarship on industries outside the north Atlantic, Anglophone sphere. While it is clear that our understanding of media industries across the world rests on studies of a select few media capitals and regions (India, China, parts of Africa, and Latin America) that attract academic interest and funding in the US and the UK, we remain optimistic about emerging and early-career scholars' commitments to de-center the Anglophone West.

Within this expanding body of scholarship, we would highlight two issues as critical for media industry scholars. In examining the business practices, strategies, and production cultures that underpin media industries' scale of operations (regional, national, global, etc.), it is crucial to steer clear of narratives of homogenization *and*, at the other extreme, celebrations of local difference. In other words, we must avoid the trap of thinking that the globalization of media industries based in Asia, for instance, implies an easy substitution of existing relations of media production and capitalist networks more generally. As Yuezhi Zhao (2003) and Govil's (2015) work in China and India respectively suggest, media industry studies needs to engage much more with histories and theories of capitalism and market cultures in order to make sense of the novel social and institutional arrangements that theories of media globalization have yet to consider. We should hasten to add that this does not imply documenting a set of practices that are somehow essentially "Indian" or "Chinese." The more relevant task is to account for the distinctive ways in which state, market, and media dynamics are worked out in relation to broader economic, political, and social formations.

If the history of media industries' formation and spatial reach is one key topic for scholars to explore further, the other related issue pertains to media convergence. Our understanding of media convergence has been shaped powerfully by Henry Jenkins's (2006) approach, which moves beyond a focus on technological dimensions to explore the industrial and cultural features of what he calls convergence culture. For Jenkins, convergence refers to "the flow of content across multiple media platforms, the cooperation between multiple media industries, and the migratory behavior of media audiences, who will go almost anywhere in search of the kinds of entertainment experiences they want" (2006, 2). Paying close attention to relations between "old" and "new" media technologies, Jenkins explores changes in the operations of the media industries in the United States as well as the ways in which participatory cultures that cohere around media and popular culture shape this rapidly evolving media terrain in important ways.

This framework for thinking about convergence is certainly useful for understanding processes of technological and industrial convergence in a range of contexts across the world. However, the pace of media development and change in Asian or African nations over the past two decades confounds notions of "old" and "new" media that inform discussions of media convergence. As Ravi Sundaram's scholarship on relations between media and urban infrastructures has shown, cultures of copying and recycling built on low-cost technologies of reproduction have, since the early 1990s, "blurred the distinctions between producers and consumers of media, adding to the diffusion of both media infrastructures – video stores, photocopy and design shops, bazaars, cable networks, piracy – and media forms (images, video, phone sms/txt, sounds)" (2009, 3). Put simply, media convergence takes different trajectories and forms in varied sociocultural contexts. The task for media industry studies scholars, then, is to situate the contemporary period of media convergence within a longer history of interrelationships between film, broadcasting, cable and satellite television, and other emergent digital media infrastructures and platforms. And more broadly, we need to deepen and refine our understanding of the interwoven histories of media and communication infrastructures, technologies, and industries and institutions in relation to, as Lisa Parks argues, "environmental, socio-economic, and geopolitical conditions" (2015, 357).

Corporate Consolidation

Although much of the deregulatory action that produced massive consolidation and conglomeration among media companies occurred in the 1980s and 1990s, the implications of these structuring adjustments were not immediately evident, and the corporations themselves required decades of internal operating adjustments to establish new norms and practices that accounted for their new scale. In many cases, the substantive shifts in ownership that involved consolidation within industries, conglomeration across industries, and established a layer of global media corporations occurred just before the long period of adjustment introduced by digital technologies.

As a result, it is often difficult to identify what bits of the contemporary political economy of any media system owe to a reconfigured ownership environment that is distinct from adaptation to digital technologies. The focus of studies of ownership are expanding from those that described the initial reconfiguration and imagined consequences (Wasko, 1994) and, in some cases, challenge assumptions that ownership scale produces consistent results. For example, research by Picard and van Weezel (2008) valuably moves beyond counting the shift from independent to chain newspaper ownership and hypothesizing or anecdotally claiming its consequences. Instead they systematically explore different forms of newspaper ownership. Notably, after trying to ground their analysis empirically, they conclude that distinctions such as being privately held versus publicly traded aren't determinant because management approach can lead to even greater variation. In some cases, chain ownership injected much-needed capital into independent papers that needed technological upgrades and were able to produce a better news product as a result. In other cases it led to the metric of constant balance sheet growth that produced short-term focus and cost cutting that undermined the news product over time. Crain (2009) investigates private equity ownership of newspapers, another type of ownership that links with those studying the implications of private equity ownership on many industries in recent decades (Appelbaum and Batt, 2014).

Grounded studies about ownership and investigations that identify whether it is particular ownership structures, management styles, metrics of industry performance, or approaches remain needed in media industry studies. The disruption faced by media organizations over the last two decades and the comparison of those that weathered adjustments for the better and worse have the potential to expand what we know, especially if we begin to explore other aspects of corporate behavior. It is likely that little can be claimed as consistently true of any ownership structure, but there is much to learn about how ownership might intersect with other features to lead more consistently to particular outcomes. For example, why is it that becoming publicly traded and the increase in private equity ownership produced such disastrous effects for newspapers, while audiovisual companies don't seem as significantly affected by the need to produce perpetual quarterly growth?

Media Industry Studies for the Next Decade

Given the centrality of the media industries to economic, political, and cultural dimensions of societies worldwide, it is not surprising that scholars from a range of disciplines are engaging with media industry studies. With this interest comes a proliferation of keywords, concepts, and frameworks from STS, management studies, economics, and more. We regard this cross-disciplinary interest as a positive development, but we would foreground "culture" as the keyword for a media industry studies rooted within the broader terrain of media studies. More broadly, in moving beyond asking why media industry studies has emerged in the last decade, what it is now, and where should it go from here, we need to consider what it can do to contribute to the current context.

For instance, how might we reflect on the stakes of studying predominantly capitalist media industries in an era of profound inequalities set in place by three to four decades of neo-liberal capitalism? What can media industry studies bring to understandings of environmental degradation? Or how can media industry studies address the environmental politics of media on topics as wide ranging as infrastructures, energy-intensive data centers that power internet-distributed media services, and rare-earth mineral mining required for the devices we use and yet quickly discard? How do we think about transnational policies and regulation that match the transnational reality of everything from content distribution to labor flows? These are central issues for many disciplines in the humanities and social sciences in the coming decades, and they have clear relevance to media industry studies.

The late 1960s, and the discord and discontent that became openly manifest at that time, are distant memories to a few and lessons in history to most of those working in the field today. Yet, there are contemporary parallels to the cultural conditions of the 1960s that could lead one to wonder whether today's questions and concerns could likewise inspire renewed and expanded investigation of the role of media institutions in the distribution and framing of ideas that are catalyzing long-simmering dissatisfaction.

Beyond these particular areas, there are opportunities for media industry studies in the next decade to explore the building of a more coherent body of knowledge and to recognize connections across media industries and move out of the largely siloed study of television, newspapers, film, recorded music, and so on. Of course, grounded studies require industry specificity, but there is value to be gained from reading widely and thinking about how particular studies inform broader knowledge about media industries generally. As we highlighted in the conclusion to the industries chapter, a rich literature exists in both film and recorded music industry scholarship about the notion of the "indie," and versions of this discussion extend into newspaper industry scholarship as well. It is valuable to contemplate corresponding insights identifiable in other industries as part of the process of specific inquiry. Of course, the dynamics never map perfectly, but such an approach may help media industry studies to expand its theoretical richness.

One of the challenges of the breadth of work that can be understood as part of the media industry studies conversation is that it encompasses a wide range of perspectives on what constitutes "good" work, or what the most important components of research might be. For some, the focus of research should be foremost about examining structures of power. This broad subfield also draws from a variety of theories to explain the operation of power that likewise can inspire disagreement. For others, grounding research in empirical evidence takes highest importance, and research that is based on rich, and perhaps novel, data takes priority. Others yet may be interested in power, but are mostly curious about cultural questions that might not be explained in terms of power. Such a perspective may prioritize more integrated research that uses industry studies alongside textual and/or audience analysis. Given this range of priorities, it can be difficult to identify an approach clearly preferable to the broad community of media industry researchers.

Collectively, we recognize value in all these approaches to media industry studies and value a lot of different work for different reasons. We have favorites characteristic of all the "levels" that organize the book, but also gravitate toward a specific register because of the questions that we find most interesting – which we also wouldn't pose as more important than others. Sometimes we value scholarship that advances a conversation by providing a very detailed explanation of the interworkings of some aspect of media industry operations, even though it may require subsequent work to tie these explanations to larger analysis and critique. We appreciate analysis that includes a high level of reflexivity about sources and analytic approaches deployed to interpret the evidence gathered, as all of this work is inevitably partial. We speak plainly of the various approaches to media industries research to encourage reflexivity and as consistent with our presentation of media industry studies as a subfield that is inclusive of a variety of approaches to examining the intersection of media industries and culture. There are many constituencies and conversations within the big tent we present. Faced with this breadth, the best strategy is to identify a scholarly conversation to which you wish to contribute, and understand what advance you offer. It is not that we do research for its own sake, but do so to expand existing understanding and to provide new insight that, in turn, helps someone else build their contribution.

References

Abel, R. (1987). *French cinema: The first wave, 1915–1929*. Princeton: Princeton University Press.

Abu-Lughod, L. (2005). *Dramas of nationhood: The politics of television in Egypt*. Chicago: University of Chicago Press.

Allen, R. C. (1980). *Vaudeville and film, 1895–1915: A study in media interaction*. New York: Arno Press.

Allen, R. C. and Gomery, D. (1985). *Film history: Theory and practice*. New York: McGraw-Hill.

Alvarado, M. and Buscombe, E. (1978). *Hazell: The making of a TV series*. London: British Film Institute.

Anderson, C. (1994). *Hollywood TV: The studio system in the fifties*. Austin: University of Texas Press.

Anderson, J. and Richie, D. (1959). *The Japanese film: Art and industry*. Rutland: Charles E. Tuttle Co.

Anderson, T. (2013). From background music to above-the-line actor: The rise of the music supervisor in converging televisual environments. *Journal of Popular Music Studies*, 25(3), 371–388.

Appelbaum, E., and Batt, R. (2014). *Private equity at work: When Wall Street manages main street*. New York: Russell Sage Foundation.

Armes, R. (1987). *Third World film making and the West*. Berkeley: University of California Press.

Athique, A., Parthasarathi, V. and Srinivas, S. (2018) *The Indian media economy*. New Delhi: Oxford University Press.

Auletta, K. (1991). *Three blind mice*. New York: Random House.

Babe, R. E. (2009). *Cultural studies and political economy: Toward a new integration*. Lanham: Lexington Books.

Bagdikian, B. H. (2004). *The new media monopoly*. Boston: Beacon Press.

Bai, R. (2005). Media commercialization, entertainment, and the party-state: The political economy of contemporary Chinese television entertainment culture. *Global Media Journal*, 4(6).

Balio, T. (1976). *United Artists: The company built by the stars*. Madison: University of Wisconsin Press.

Balio, T. (1987). *United Artists, Volume 2, 1951–1978: The company that changed the film industry*. Madison: University of Wisconsin Press.

Balio, T., ed. (1990). *Hollywood in the age of television*. Boston: Unwin Hyman.

Banks, M. J. (2015). *The writers: A history of American screenwriters and their guild*. New Brunswick: Rutgers University Press.

Banks, M., Conor, B. and Mayer, V. (2015). *Production studies, the sequel!: cultural studies of global media industries*. New York: Routledge.

Barnett, K. (2014). Talent scouts in US recording industry. In Johnson, D., Kompare, D., and Santo, A., eds., *Making media work: Cultures of management in the entertainment industries,* 1st edn. New York: New York University Press, pp. 113–141.

Baym, N. (2018). *Playing to the crowd: Musicians, audiences, and the intimate work of connection*. New York: New York University Press.

Becker, R. (2006). *Gay TV and straight America*. New Brunswick: Rutgers University Press.

Biskind, P. (2004). *Down and dirty pictures: Miramax, Sundance and the rise of independent film*. New York: Simon and Schuster.

Boczkowski, P. (2004). *Digitizing the news: Innovation in online newspapers*. Cambridge: MIT Press.

Boddy, W. (1993). *Fifties television: The industry and its critics*. Urbana: University of Illinois Press.

Bordwell, D., Staiger, J. and Thompson, K. (1985). *The classical Hollywood cinema: Film style and mode of production to 1960*. New York: Columbia University Press.

Born, G. (2004). *Uncertain vision: Birt, Dyke and the reinvention of the BBC*. London: Secker and Warburg.

Bourdieu, P. (1984). *Distinction: A social critique of the judgement of taste*. Cambridge: Harvard University Press.

Boyd-Barrett, O. (1977). Media imperialism: Towards an international framework for the analysis of media systems. In Curran, J., Gurevitch, M., and Woollacott, J., eds., *Mass communication and society,* 1st edn. London: Edward Arnold, pp. 116–135.

Boyle, R. (2018). *The talent industry: Television, cultural intermediaries and new digital pathways*. Cham: Springer.

Brunsdon, C. and Morley, D. G. (1978). *Everyday television: Nationwide*. London: British Film Institute.

Burns, T. (1977). *The BBC: Public institution and private world*. London: Macmillan.

Caldwell, J. T. (1995). *Televisuality: Style, crisis, and authority in American television*. New Brunswick: Rutgers University Press.

Caldwell, J. T. (2006). Cultural studies of media production: Critical industrial practices. In White, M. and Schwoch, J., eds., *Questions of method in cultural studies*, 1st edn. Malden: Blackwell, pp. 109–153.

Holt, J. and Perren, A. (2009). *Media industries: History, theory, and method.* Oxford: Wiley-Blackwell.

Horkheimer, M. and Adorno, T. W. (2002) [1944]. The culture industry: Enlightenment as mass deception. In *Dialectic of enlightenment. Philosophical fragments.* Trans. by Jephcott, E. Stanford: Stanford University Press, pp. 94–136

Innis, H. (1950). *Empire and communications.* Oxford: Clarendon.

Innis, H. (1951). *The bias of communication.* Toronto: University of Toronto Press.

Iwabuchi, K. (2010). Globalization, East Asian media cultures and their publics. *Asian Journal of Communication,* 20(2), 197–212.

Jäckel, A. (2003). *European film industries.* London: British Film Institute.

Jenkins, H. (2006). *Convergence Culture: Where Old and New Media Collide.* New York: New York University Press.

Johnson, R. (1986). What is cultural studies anyway? *Social Text,* 16, 38–80.

Juul, J. (2010). *A casual revolution: Reinventing video games and their players.* Cambridge: MIT press.

Kaposi, I. (2001). Voices from the Hungarian edge. *Open Democracy.*

Keane, M. (2015). *The Chinese television industry.* London: British Film Institute.

Kemper, T. (2009). *Hidden talent: The emergence of Hollywood agents.* Berkeley: University of California Press.

Kerr, A. (2017). *Global games: Production, circulation and policy in the networked era.* London: Routledge.

Khalil, J. and Kraidy, M. (2017). *Arab television industries.* London: Bloomsbury Publishing.

King, G. (2005). *American independent cinema.* London: IB Tauris.

Kracauer, S. (1947). *From Caligari to Hitler: A psychological study of the German film.* Princeton: Princeton University Press.

Kraidy, M. (2005). *Hybridity, or the cultural logic of globalization.* Philadelphia: Temple University Press.

Krings, M. and Okome, O. (2013). *Global Nollywood: The transnational dimensions of an African video film industry.* Bloomington: Indiana University Press.

Kumar, S. (2006). *Gandhi meets primetime: Globalization and nationalism in Indian television.* Urbana: University of Illinois Press.

Larkin, B. (2008). *Signal and noise: Media, infrastructure, and urban culture in Nigeria.* Durham: Duke University Press.

Lent, J. A. (1978). *Broadcasting in Asia and the Pacific: A continental survey of radio and television.* Philadelphia: Temple University Press.

Levine, E. (2001). Toward a paradigm for media production research: Behind the scenes at General Hospital. *Critical Studies in Media Communication,* 18(1), 66–82.

Lewis, J. (1997). *Whom God wishes to destroy: Francis Coppola and the new Hollywood.* Durham: Duke University Press.

Lobato, R., 2012. *Shadow economies of cinema: Mapping informal film distribution.* Bloomsbury Publishing.

Lobato, R. and Thomas, J. (2015). *The informal media economy.* Cambridge: Polity.

Lotz, A. and Newcomb, H. (2012). The production of media fiction. In Jensen, K., ed., *A handbook of media and communication research,* 2nd edn. New York: Routledge, pp. 71–86.

Lotz, A. D. (2006). *Redesigning women: Television after the network era.* Urbana: University of Illinois Press.

Lotz, A. D. (2018). *We now disrupt this broadcast: How cable transformed television and the internet revolutionized it all.* Cambridge: MIT Press.

Mankekar, P. (1999). *Screening culture, viewing politics: An ethnography of television, womanhood, and nation in postcolonial India.* Durham: Duke University Press.

Martin Jr., A. L. (2018). Introduction: What is queer production studies/why is queer production studies? *Journal of Film and Video,* 70(3–4), 3–7.

Martin Jr., A. L. (2015). Scripting black gayness: Television authorship in black-cast sitcoms. *Television and New Media,* Vol. 16(7), 648–663.

Mattelart, A. (1976). Cultural imperialism in the multinationals' age. *Instant Research on Peace and Violence,* 6 (4), 160–174.

Mattelart, A. (1979). *Multinational corporations and the control of culture: The ideological apparatuses of imperialism.* Brighton: Harvester.

Mattelart, A. and Dorfman, A. (1975) *How to read Donald Duck: Imperialist ideology in the Disney comic.* New York: International General.

Mayer, V. (2011). *Below the line: Producers and production studies in the new television economy.* Durham: Duke University Press.

Mayer, V., Banks, M. and Caldwell, J. T. (2009). *Production studies: Cultural studies of media industries.* New York: Routledge.

Mazzarella, W. (2003). *Shoveling smoke: Advertising and globalization in contemporary India.* Durhamwi: Duke University Press.

McChesney, R. W. (1997). *Corporate media and the threat to democracy.* New York: Seven Stories Press.

McChesney, R. W. (2001). Policing the unthinkable. *Open Democracy.*

McDonald, P. (2013). *Hollywood stardom.* Oxford: Wiley-Blackwell.

Meehan, E. (1983). Neither heroes nor villains: Toward a political economy of the rating industry. PhD Dissertation. The University of Illinois at Urbana-Champaign.

Metz, C. (1974). *Film language: A semiotics of the cinema.* Chicago: University of Chicago Press.

Miège, B. (1987). The logics at work in the new cultural industries. *Media, Culture and Society,* 9(3), 273–289.

Miège, B. (2011). Theorizing the cultural industries: Persistent specificities and reconsiderations. In Wasko, J., Murdock, G., and Sousa, H., eds., *The handbook of political economy of communication.* Malden, MA: Wiley-Blackwell.

Mihelj, S. and Huxtable, S. (2018). *From media systems to media cultures: Understanding socialist television.* Cambridge: Cambridge University Press.

Miller, J. (2012). Global Nollywood: The Nigerian movie industry and alternative global networks in production and distribution. *Global Media and Communication,* 8(2), 117–133.

Miller, T., Govil, N., McMurria, J. and Maxwell, R. (2001). *Global Hollywood.* London: British Film Institute.

Morley, D. (1980). *The "Nationwide" audience: Structure and decoding.* London: British Film Institute.

Morley, D. and Robins, K. (1995). *Spaces of identity.* New York: Routledge.

Mosco, V. (2009). *The political economy of communication,* 2nd edn. London: Sage.

Mulvey, L. (1975). Visual pleasure and narrative cinema. *Screen.* 16(3), 6–18.

Murdock, G. and Golding, P. (1973). For a political economy of mass communications. *Socialist Register,* 10(10).

Musser, C. (1990). *The emergence of cinema: The American screen to 1907.* Berkeley: University of California Press.

Negus, K. (1992). *Producing pop: Culture and conflict in the popular music industry.* London: E. Arnold.

Negus, K. (1999). *Music genres and corporate cultures.* London: Routledge.

Newcomb, H. and Alley, R. (1983). *The producer's medium: Conversations with creators of America's leading television producers.* Oxford: Oxford University Press.

Newman, M. (2011). *Indie: An American film culture.* New York: Columbia University Press.

Nguyen-Thu, G. (2018). *Television in post-reform Vietnam: Nation, media, market.* New York: Routledge.

O'Donnell, C. (2014). *Developer's dilemma: The secret world of videogame creators.* Cambridge: MIT Press.

Ortner, S. (2013). *Not Hollywood: Independent film at the twilight of the American dream.* Durham: Duke University Press.

Ortner, S. B. (2009). Studying sideways: Ethnographic access in Hollywood. In Mayer, V., Banks, M., and Caldwell, J. T., eds., *Production studies,* 1st edn. New York: Routledge, pp. 183–197.

Owen, B. and Wildman, S. (1992). *Video economics.* Cambridge: Harvard University Press.

Parks, L. (2018) Industries and infrastructures. Media in Transition Conference. Utrecht University, Netherlands.

Parks, L. (2015). Stuff you can kick: Toward a theory of media infrastructures. In Svensson, Patrik and Goldberg, David Theo, eds., *Between the humanities and the digital.* Cambridge: MIT Press.

Parks, L. and Starosielski, N. (2015). *Signal traffic: Critical studies of media infrastructures,* 1st edn. Urbana: University of Illinois Press.

Parks, L. and Kumar, S. (2002). *Planet TV: A global television reader.* New York: New York University Press.

Paterson, C., Lee, D., Saha, A., and Zoellner, A. (2016). *Advancing media production research: Shifting sites, methods, and politics.* London: Springer.

Pendakur, M. (1985). Dynamics of cultural policy making: The US film industry in India, *Journal of Communication,* 35, 52–72.

Perren, A. (2012). *Indie, inc.: Miramax and the transformation of Hollywood in the 1990s.* Austin: University of Texas Press.

Peterson, R. (1982). Five constraints on the production of culture: Law, technology, market, organizational structure and occupational careers. *Journal of Popular Culture,* 16(2), 143–152.

Peterson, R. and Anand, N. (2004). The production of culture perspective. *Annual Review of Sociology*, 30, 311–344.

Petre, C. (2015). The traffic factories: Metrics at chartbeat, gawker media, and *The New York Times. Tow Center for Digital Journalism.*

Picard, R. (2002). *The economics and financing of media companies.* New York: Fordham.

Picard, R. G. and van Weezel, A. (2008). Capital and control: Consequences of different forms of newspaper ownership. *The International Journal on Media Management*, 10(1), 22–31.

Pillai, S. (2015). *Madras studios: Narrative, genre, and ideology in Tamil cinema.* New Delhi: Sage Publications India.

Powdermaker, H. (1950). *Hollywood, the dream factory: An anthropologist looks at the movie-makers.* Boston: Little, Brown and Company.

Punathambekar, A. (2013). *From Bombay to Bollywood: The making of a global media industry.* New York: New York University Press.

Redvall, E. (2013). *Writing and producing television drama in Denmark: From the Kingdom to The Killing.* New York: Springer.

Reese, S. (2009). Managing the symbolic arena: The media sociology of Herbert Gans. In Holtz-Bacha C., Reus G., Becker L.B., eds., *Wissenschaft mit Wirkung*, 1st edn. VS Verlag für Sozialwissenschaften, pp. 279–293.

Richie, D. (1971). *Japanese cinema: Film style and national character.* Garden City: Doubleday.

Rivero, Y. M. (2015). *Broadcasting modernity: Cuban commercial television, 1950–1960.* Durham: Duke University Press.

Robinson, S. (2011). Convergence crises: News work and news space in the digitally transforming newsroom. *Journal of Communication*, 61, 1122–1141.

Rosten, L. (1941). *Hollywood: The movie colony, the movie makers.* New York: Harcourt, Brace, and co.

Roussel, V. (2017). *Representing talent: Hollywood agents and the making of movies.* Chicago: University of Chicago Press.

Saha, A. (2011). Negotiating the third space: British Asian independent record labels and the cultural politics of difference. *Popular Music and Society*, 34(4), 437–454.

Saha, A. (2018). *Race and the cultural industries.* Cambridge: Polity.

Sarwar, B. (2001). The media in Pakistan: a new era? *Open Democracy.*

Scannell, P. (2007). *Media and communication.* London: Sage.

Scannell, P. and Cardiff, D. (1991). *A social history of British broadcasting. 1. 1922–1939, serving the nation.* Oxford: Blackwell.

Schatz, T. (1988). *The genius of the system: Hollywood filmmaking in the studio era.* New York: Pantheon.

Schiller, H. (1969). *Mass communications and American empire.* Boston: Beacon Press.

Schiller, H. (1976). *Communication and cultural domination.* New York: Sharpe.

Schiller, H. (1992). *Mass communication and American empire*, 2nd edn. Boulder: Westview.

Schlesinger, P. (1978). *Putting reality together: The BBC Newsroom.* London: Constable.

Schramm, W. (1964). Book review of the month: Who is to know?: Mass media and national development: The role of information in the developing countries. *American Behavioral Scientist*, 8(3), 19–20.

Seaver, N. (2018) Captivating algorithms: Recommender systems as traps. *Journal of Material Culture*.

Sender, K. (2005). *Business, not politics: The making of the gay market*. New York: Columbia University Press.

Sinclair, J. (1986). Dependent development and broadcasting: The Mexican formula. *Media, Culture and Society*, 8(1), 81–101.

Smythe, D. (1977). Communications: blindspot of western Marxism. *Canadian Journal of Political and Social Theory*, 1(3), 1–27.

Smythe, D. W. (1981). On the audience commodity and its work. In Durham, M. G. and Kellner, D. M., eds., *Media and cultural studies*, 1st edn. Malden: Blackwell, pp. 230–256.

Spigel, L. (1992). *Make room for TV: Television and the family ideal in postwar America*. Chicago: University of Chicago Press.

Srinivas, S. V. (2013). *Politics as performance: A social history of the Telugu cinema*. New Delhi: Permanent Black.

Straubhaar, J. (1991). Beyond media imperialism: Asymmetrical interdependence and cultural proximity. *Critical Studies in Mass Communication*, 8(1), 39–59.

Straubhaar, J. D. (2007). *World television: From global to local*. London: Sage.

Street, S. (1997). *British national cinema*. London: Routledge.

Sullivan, J. (2009). Leo C. Rosten's Hollywood: power, status, and the primacy of economic and social networks in cultural production. In Mayer, V., Banks, M., and Caldwell, J. T., eds., *Production studies*, 1st edn. New York: Routledge, pp. 47–61.

Sundaram, R. (2009). *Pirate modernity: Delhi's media urbanism*. New Delhi: Routledge.

Szczepanik, P. and Vonderau, P. (2013). *Behind the screen: Inside European production cultures*. New York: Palgrave Macmillan.

Tartikoff, B. and Leerhsen, C. (1993). *The last great ride*. New York: Delta.

Taylor, T. L. (2018). *Watch me play: Twitch and the rise of game live streaming*. Princeton: Princeton University Press.

Thompson, J. (2013). *Merchants of culture: the publishing business in the twenty-first century*. Cambridge: Polity.

Tinic, S. (2005). *On location: Canada's television industry in a global market*. Toronto: University of Toronto Press.

Tomlinson, J. (1999). *Globalization and culture*. London: Polity.

Tuchman, G. (1978). *Making news: A study in the construction of reality*. New York: Free Press.

Tunstall, J. (1991). A media industry perspective. *Annals of the International Communication Association*, 14(1), 163–186.

Turner, G. (1990). Representing the nation. In Bennett, T., ed., *Popular fiction: Technology, ideology, production, reading*. London: Routledge.

Turow, J. (1982). Unconventional programs on commercial television: An organizational perspective. Ettema, J. S. and Whitney, D. C., eds., *Individuals in mass media organizations: Creativity and constraint*. Thousand Oaks: Sage.

Turow, J. (1992). The organizational underpinnings of contemporary media conglomerates. *Communication Research*, 19(6), 682–704.

Tussey, E. (2018). *The procrastination economy: The big business of downtime.* New York: New York University Press.

Tzioumakis, Y. (2006). Marketing David Mamet: Institutionally assigned film authorship in contemporary American cinema. *The Velvet Light Trap*, 57(1), 60–75.

Varis, T. (1973). *International inventory of television programme structure and the flow of TV programmes between nations* (Report of a Research Project Supported by UNESCO). Tampere: University of Tampere.

Warner, K. (2015). *The cultural politics of colorblind TV casting.* New York: Routledge.

Wasko, J. (1982). *Movies and money: Financing the American film industry.* Norwood: Ablex Publishing.

Wasko, J. (1994). *Hollywood in the information age: Beyond the silver screen.* Cambridge: Polity Press.

Wikström, P. (2013). *The music industry: Music in the cloud*, 2nd edn. Cambridge: Polity.

Wikström, P. (2020). *The music industry: Music in the cloud*, 3rd edn. Cambridge: Polity.

Williams, R. (1979). *Politics and letters.* London: New Left Books.

Wollen, P. (1972). *Signs and meaning in the cinema.* New and enlarged. Bloomington: Indiana University Press.

Wuest, B. (2018). A shelf of one's own: A queer production studies approach to LGBT film distribution and categorization. *Journal of Film and Video*, 70(3–4), 24–43.

Wyatt, J. (1994). *High concept: Movies and marketing in Hollywood.* Austin: University of Texas Press.

Wyatt, J. (1996). Economic constraints/economic opportunities: Robert Altman as auteur. *Velvet Light Trap*, 38, 51–68.

Zhao, Y. (2003). Transnational capital, the Chinese state, and China's communication industries in a fractured society. *The Public/Javnost*, 10(4), 53–73.

Index